This is why you

know me.

-Maxwell R. Shultz

"This is why you know me."
Written and experienced by Maxwell Shultz

The title started as a joke that stuck, and it was held
between Me, Ben Bunker, and Bill M.

Cover art by Brian Canty
www.brianrcanty.com (Don't forget the 'r' in the middle!)

Headshot by Shivohn Fleming

The events described happened between April and July
2015. For privacy reasons, some names and occupations
have been changed.

Edited by Heather Turrell

I'd like to offer a very special thank you to my friends and
family that helped me with this, and to the special
characters that made each and every one of these stories
as real as they are.

This project is dedicated to
Mom.

Mom as in my great grandmother, not mother. Also, as in the title for the 20th chapter. Her chapter was the first of these essays I wrote.

Thank you for everything,
Mom.

7. Nineteen

12. An Easy Start

18. Smoke Barbeque

32. Over Near Tennessee

41. Andy In Atlanta

50. Fair Enough

59. The Saggy State

70. Still Sagging

80. A Very Proud Red Hippie

86. Pixie and the Pot

96. Turn Around!

113. Mid-day Parade

122. Mr. Rodgers in Tokyo

129. Adobe the Beautiful

137. Cookie

152. Alone

154. It's a Plain, Dry Death

158. Technology

162. Ten Kids and Counting

167. Mom

183. Fare-Thee-Well

Nineteen

A few weeks ago I lied to my favorite author. I didn't do it maliciously, but when David Sedaris signed my favorite piece of writing, his *Smoking Section*, I told him I don't smoke. I thought I had quit the compulsive habit, but here, now, I'm at my dresser and ashing into my tray for the umpteenth time today. My friend Mike introduced me to cigarettes on a summer night when I was nineteen. The first pack I bought were yellow American Spirits; the eleven dollars per-pack intimidated me. I needed a stress relief and Mike knew weed wasn't enough. We walked to a dock and smoked and talked about life for hours. I'd just ended the first serious romantic relationship of my life and was suffering a terrible depression over it. I know that the excuse is an overused one, but it's mine. If you are or ever have been a smoker, you know smoking is one of the best and one of the worst decisions you can make.

****

I was nineteen when I was eating breakfast with a friend named Phil, and I discovered, undoubtedly, that I was not a heterosexual. It was one of those situations where I found myself in conversation with my friend, and thinking to myself, "I would really like to see him naked." Many people have that notion throughout their life about certain people; this time, however, was the first time it was with a good friend, but also the first time I had these feelings for a man. I knew the situation was bad when it was my turn to speak and I had no idea what he had been talking about. I made up some excuse to leave, saying I had to go to work, and once away from it all, I panicked. Like most people I know who realize something like this about themselves I tried to deny it for a long time. Very quickly, my feelings for that friend did go away, but I started noticing men the way I'd noticed girls in middle school.

I was still very attracted to women, usually much more so than men, so I knew that I was not totally homosexual either. Bi-sexual sounded nice, but a little too exclusive. If you're

8

going to be into men and women, why exclude gender queer people, transsexuals, or anyone else. After some research and talking to people in the same situation I began to identify myself as a pansexual. Merriam-Webster defines pansexual as, "exhibiting or implying many forms of sexual expression." To me that term means being attracted to someone's personality and expressions much more than their body or what's between their legs. I am far more attracted to someone if they can hold a strong conversation with me than if they have a ripped body or watermelon tits.

****

At nineteen, I should've been living the dream; I'd begun to have some local success at stand-up comedy, and was running my own radio show for the college I attended in Lowell, MA. Some friends I'd met there are like family now, but going to college at that point didn't really agree with me. I was never financially stable enough to not have to work almost full time. I was also unable to move out of my parents' house. I was constantly under great stress. By the time I was twenty, I dropped out, but was still able to keep my show. I began putting most of my time into delivering pizza for Domino's to save some quick money so I could get out of town and clear my head for a while.

I met a friend at work, named Jon, who introduced me to the world of Couchsurfing.com. The site works a lot like a dating website. You make a profile for yourself, and explain what you're looking for, just not in a lover, but in a traveling experience. If you and the other person get along, as a traveler, he or she will opt to host you on their couch or floor for a day or two in exchange for favors. Something like making dinner or driving someone to work would count, but no actual currency is exchanged. It's a very useful tool. I fell in love with the idea, saved up my money and bought a tan, rusty, and overall beat up 1996 Toyota Camry. Its radio was very strange because although it didn't have a CD player, it did have an AUX input alongside a tape player. It had brown fabric seats, leaked gas, and worked as my home. I decided to spend my next several months driving, sleeping in strange homes, and doing comedy open mics nationwide!

An Easy Start

When I left my parent's house in Haverhill, Massachusetts, I started to play Alexandru Sabau's album, "In Between the Standing Trees," which he had personally given to me at an open mic. It is still one of my favorite folk albums and would go on to be the backing tracks for a large chunk of the trip. Ironically the opening line is, *"Headin' back home..."* My first few stops were visiting some friends in southern Massachusetts and in Connecticut.

I celebrated 420, the marijuana smoker's holiday, with my friend Jermichael. I got so high that I vomited, a lot. I decided to go to sleep, opened Jermichael's bedroom door, and destroyed his trash can. The first time I got that high was in Lowell, Mass. I got stoned at a friend of a friend's house, and I guess the mix of weed wasn't working for me and I threw up all over the poor guy's shower. I cleaned what I could with most of his toilet paper, and ran the shower for the rest, which included a floor mat.

I took almost an hour to clean it up, then told them I had to leave. Although there was no mess left behind, I still feel bad that they have no idea about it. I then walked half a mile and performed a college radio program.

****

Later on, I found myself at my friend Mike's grandmother's condo in Guilford Connecticut. Immediately, we started talking about open mics and his, then girlfriend, Joyce. The only time I saw her on that stay, was when she and her friends came to meet up with Mike and me at a park. One of them came up to us and asked us very kindly if we wanted some of his cocaine. We politely declined, but walked with them as several of the group members snorted the powdery drug. Later, at one of their apartments, the coke came back out and again, we were offered some. We declined again, only to watch a man dip his cigarette in the cocaine, the same way they did in old movies with the tip of the cigarette, where the tobacco pokes out, now coated in coke. He lit the cigarette and it exploded in front of him nearly half way up the butt. He laughed. I said, "Now I really don't want any." I listened as three different people, at different times, said phrases along the lines of, "You know, I want to go into the Army, I've thought about it and that's the branch of the military I want to go into. But, I just love doing drugs so much. I'd rather just do drugs my whole life than fight for the country." The other two people said the same thing about college and getting a job.

Toward the end of my stay, I picked up a cassette copy of Tom Petty's *Full Moon Fever* and it, along with Alex's record, would be a significant part of the tracking for my trip. Just before my departure to New York, Mike pulled me aside, handed me the third and final major soundtrack to my trip, and said "I know it's not your style, but I want you to have this and promise to listen to it." The tape was Dr. Dre's 1992 album, *The Chronic*. These three albums were the majority of the music I listened to during my trip.

****

I drove clear past the city, and up north to Binghamton, New York, to meet with my Aunt Judy and Uncle Brian. Unfortunately, Uncle Brian was at the age where dementia was beginning to set in a little. He seemed to make light of it. I'm not sure if he did this to get a raise out of people, but when someone asked him something from an old memory, his catch phrase seemed to always be, with a smile, "I couldn't tell ya!" The man does remember important things though; when driving through town, he often pointed to things like bridges and major roadways and said, "That's my bridge, still standing." Aunt Judy and I became close over our beliefs in a potential afterlife, though differing on religious beliefs. She was a Priest and I didn't have any religious affiliation. After a few days there, I drove to my grandparent's condo in Reading, Pennsylvania.

****

I was closer with my grandparents than I was with most family members. My grandmother, whom I called granum, worked for a sportswear company and with conference calls. She tended to handle finances, and overall was the sensible one of the relationship. She is a shorter woman, and is overall in very good shape. My grandfather. on the other hand, is kind of in his own world a lot of the time. He was known to come up with crackpot ideas all the time, and is a great storyteller. He lost his left ear a while ago and if you don't know why, he will ask you, "Do you want the real story, or a good story?" Regardless of what you tell him you want, he would go on with something like this, "There I was, ready to go, and the French Foreign Legion shot it clean off!" In reality, he surgically lost it to skin cancer. He is also the tallest and frailest member of my father's side of the family. They've always welcomed me with open arms, accepting and encouraging nearly everything I did. For example, when my parents found out I smoked weed, they sat me down and demanded to know everything about my habit. My mother went on to assume I was doing damn near all other hard drugs for years. My grandmother, however, said "Yeah, well who hasn't?"

I visited my great grandmother twice on that visit. We called her "Mom." Seeing Mom twice in one visit, was a very strange and wonderful thing to happen; sometimes a year would pass without me seeing her. Before I left for the rest of the country, I showed my grandfather my comedy album. He was the first family member to hear my material in length. He told me he'd let me know what he thought of it after a few good listens. I hugged him, hugged Granum, and put my things in the car. As they waved me off, I called my aunt and uncle in Annapolis, to tell them I'd be on my way. I was on my way to displaying my comedy across the country, to strange family members' homes, and to even stranger strangers' homes. I was on my way to an adventure.

Smoke Barbeque

Part One:

My Uncle Chris had a mysterious job, kind of like the character Chandler Bing. I knew he was very successful at whatever it was, but the actual job was never explained to me. While at a baseball game at the Naval Academy in Annapolis, I learned that Chris was an important figure for a toy company, and traveled often for it. My cousins got bored and went off on their own. My 12 year old cousin, Ian, was wandering with an adorable crush of his, and his younger sister, Helen, was wishing to be doing literally anything that wasn't watching a baseball game in the heat.

My uncle blew me away about his kids' educations. Ian, in the sixth grade, is now fluent in French. Helen, accidentally following my footsteps, can't retain a foreign language to save her wits. They've always been some of the more well-off members of the family, but private schooling like this astounded me. I laughed when Ian tried speaking to me in French, and I remembered my own sister, of the same age as Ian, being shocked to learn that I would not in fact leave the country when I went to New Orleans. These things in mind, I decided that it was time to play more open mics.

After looking for places to perform in Maryland, I came across "Smoke BBQ," a general open mic location in Bethesda. Although I know nothing about it, yes, I was in the town where many famous video games are made. From Annapolis, I had about a forty-five minute drive ahead of me. Had it been nearby I may not have gone inside. Smoke BBQ is a bar, which are wonderful for musicians, for drinkers, and for lonely bedmates. Historically, they are ghastly for public speakers. It's the nature of the beast, drunks usually don't want to stop their conversations to watch someone else speak, especially at eleven at night.

When I walked in, a mid-height and well-built man introduced himself to me as Mike. He was running the show and seemed excited to see me perform. He wanted to make sure I stuck around to see his band end the night. When I showed up, two men were playing folky covers of early 2000's pop tunes, like "All Star" and "Chasing Cars." They were very talented; midway through their set, Mike told me I would be performing after a man named Zach, which meant, including the men playing now, I would be on in three acts.

I took a seat and worked on my setlist for that evening. As the next performer began to strum his guitar, I realized that not only was this 50-year-old slob probably playing the guitar for the first time ever, he was also unable to sit on his stool. This wasn't because he was too into the music and I don't think it really had much to do with his drunk ass either, but rather because he used his entire body to change chords, to pluck strings, and to sing. Single handedly, this buffoon had driven out over half of the crowded bar. He continued to play for well over 20 minutes. The only redeemable part of his set was his sloppy cover of Russell Brand's "Inside You" from Forgetting Sarah Marshal. It's silly that anyone would cover that song. About two 'songs' into the man's set, Zach came over to me; now I would actually meet the legend. Zach is a six-foot-five thin black man. He wears a fancy hat; on the brim, is a lightning bolt earring, which he treats like bangs that are just a little too long. He has a voice like a speed induced Michael Stipe and when I told him I was playing after him, he eccentrically introduced himself.

"I'm Zach Lightning! I hear you're doing comedy, right man? That's awesome man! Do what you love; but listen, I hate amateur comedians. I'm going to leave during your set, but do your thing. I have several records available, look me up sometime. I love playing my music here, it's such a good environment!"

While I waited to perform, Zach wandered around talking to other people. A blonde woman with blue eyes, around my age, was looking me over from across the bar; she was with a man, so I paid little attention to her. Once Zach got up on the stage and plugged his guitar in, I quickly learned that he is the embodiment of a black Berlin-Bowie era B-side performer. The music, all original, was very good, but repetitive and almost like it was from Mars. He was interesting to watch, in a very good way. Unfortunately, he drove more people out of the already nearly vacant bar.

I knew it was my turn to talk in front of an almost empty bar. However, against the odds, by the time my second story had begun, I had brought at least twenty-five people from the street to listen to me. They were glued to my jokes and stories. Even those sitting on stools at the bar had turned to watch me go on for nearly a half hour, and Zach Lightening had not left either; he was hooked. By the time I had finished my set, they only wanted more.

Mike came up to me immediately while the next act was setting up.

"How long are you in town? If you come by tomorrow night, I guarantee you a spot in the lineup and a bigger audience. My band is headlining a show here and we want you back."
"I'm only in town for another day and a half or so, but I'll see. Thanks so much!"

Zach then approached me with the line, "You are the first comedian I've enjoyed at an open mic in years. Keep going!" He continued, "I used to do stand-up when I lived in LA. I was in college out there, man, LA is unlike any other place. My roommate was a childhood friend of mine, right, but he had converted to Scientology. I didn't know anything about it, right, so I supported his religious choice, whatever. But then it got crazy, he started to wake me up in the middle of the night, other scientologists would bang on my walls, they wanted to freak me out, convert me. I had to get out man, shit was crazy."

Something got us off topic and Zach said, "Wait do you..." He pressed his thumb and index finger together, brought them to his mouth, inhaled, leaned way back, and wheezed. I nodded yes, and he loudly whispered, "Aw shit! Let's go!"

After hearing him so far, I don't know why I found myself sprinting with Zach to his car, parked way down the main road. Once in his car, he packed and passed me the bowl, then started to go over what he already told me about LA. Then added,

"You know that Travolta movie where he plays Clinton? They paid for that one. Scientology is the only recognized religion to be paid for and to use blackmail to become recognized. Man, the first time I tripped, on acid, was with my old roommate. It was great! One of my best trips, but I didn't know, until later, that he tripped with me because you need to open your mind to be in the religion! It freaked me the fuck out, man. Damn, you know, I can't go back to LA or they'll get me. I'm not supposed to be in the state of California."
To break my silence, I told him that I was all set when he went to pass the bowl again. Realizing I was damn well stoned, Zach said,

"Alright, well let's go!" And again, we sprinted back to Smoke BBQ. Once inside, I realized I had missed Mike's band, and he looked at me, then Zach, then me again and in a disappointed and sarcastic tone said, "You went to his car, didn't you?"

Part Two:

After a good night's sleep and talking with my uncle about the night before, I decided I had to return, if only to make sure the place really existed and I didn't just imagine the whole weird night. I spent my day mostly in their yard with the dogs, playing catch and fetch, which eventually transpired into a water balloon fight with all of us. All the while I was working out what different material I would return with, and considering the possibility that I dreamt the whole night, and the place would be a huge CVS or something now. This concern is one I still hold to this day about Smoke BBQ and my eventual return.

By the time I did return, the show was around its midpoint. Mike came right to me, shook my hand and said,

"Great! I'm so happy you're back. I'll fit you in similarly to last night, okay? The duo from last night's on now, then Zach, then you. Sound good?"

"Sure man, thanks!"

"Yup, my band's on at the end, so two after you, my friend."

Then Zach came up, "Yo man! You're here! Wanna smoke?"

"I don't before I perform, but maybe after, man."

"Aw shit! You're going up again, awesome! Alright!"

He was wearing almost the exact same clothing from the night before, hat and all, and he turned from me to start talking to a woman around his age. I did my best to play the wing man for him, and it seemed to work. I think they slept together that night, which seemed strange because Zach didn't seem like any sort of ladies man. As I let him flirt more, I sat to finish my set for the night, and the same girl from the previous night was looking at me with the sex eye from across the bar. She was alone this time, but I was focused on what I was doing more than her. Caution went to the wind though when she left to smoke a cigarette. They're horrible things, but wonderful social excuses to talk to someone. I noticed that she was also a little shorter than me. I went out, lit my American Spirit, and started talking to her.

"Didn't I see you last night?" I said to her.

She replied in a shy innocent way, "Yeah I think you did. I saw you here."

"Weren't you with a guy? Where'd he go?"

"No, I wasn't. Well, I guess, sorta, but it's my, umm, brother."

"Oh okay. You seemed to be looking at me from across the room, yeah? I'm Max"

"Yeah, I guess, I was, I don't know," she blushed, "You're kinda cute. And I'm Molly"

"So are you! I'm performing in a bit if you'd like to stick around."

"Yeah sure!"

I tossed my butt into the street, and we kissed to Zach Lightning's music.

****

When it was my turn to get on stage, though, Molly was nowhere to be found, she had left. Zach, however, was right in front of me, urging me on further into my stories. The crowd did love me for the second time in a row, and it was a full house. I went on again for about a half hour, of all material they had not yet heard, and even was found telling people who were talking at the bar to "shut the fuck up," because, "I'm talking up here!" After that, even they were glued to me. That's a feeling difficult to replicate.

When my set finished, Zach Lightning had moved from in front of me, to behind the bar to smoke a butt. Molly had reappeared from the bathroom now, and apologized for missing my set, "I was on the phone, with, umm, my mom."

"Oh it's alright, if you'd like, I can hangout tomorrow before I get out of town. May I have your number?"

"What if you just give me yours and I'll think about it?"

This seemed like a trap, but as a comedian, I had to see where it led me. "Sure," I said, and put it into her phone. She then left, just as fast as she came. Mike's band had begun to play now, and they were a weird acoustic heavy metal band that played covers of folk songs. It wasn't bad music, they're all talented, but when Mike started to trudge out Tom Petty's *Last Dance with Mary Jane*, I was a little put off. Of course, when they finished, I shook his hand, and said I was shocked to hear that they played such unique music.

"Thanks man for sticking around! I know you've got to go in the morning, but anytime, anytime at all you want to come back we'll be here. Maybe I can meet you on the road someplace too! Who knows what'll happen, but we love you here, man!"

"Thanks, I do have to get out of here, but it's truly been a pleasure to come back. Do you know where Zach went? I'd like to say see you later to him."

"Check out back, I'm not sure though."

When I went to the back of the bar, outside, I found two employees smoking cigarettes and talking about the night. They tossed Zach's name out there, and I asked where he went, "He was just here talking to us! I, I don't know! Maybe he's in the bathroom or some shit."

He wasn't, and part of me does believe Zach either isn't real or evaporated in his own lightning. Either way, I never saw him again.

****

Once back at my aunt and uncle's, I packed my things, and tried to go to sleep. The next morning, I had to head down South, through the Carolinas, and eventually to Georgia. Around three in the morning, though, Molly texted me, claiming her name was not in fact Molly, but rather Polly. She said I must have misheard her; I didn't. She asked for a photo of me, but when I asked for one back, after a struggle, it was of a very different woman.

The photos exchanged were not sexual at all, I sent her a photo of my face and only wanted one back. When I met this girl she had pale skin, blue eyes, and light brown hair. The woman in the photo had olive skin, green eyes, and nearly black hair. She insisted that I mustn't remember correctly. Polly also mentioned that she couldn't hang out the following morning, but really wanted to have sex. It went into total and absolute hysteria. Not only did she claim I was shy and awkward, but wished I had asked so she could have "fucked you (me) right there in an alley." This quickly turned into wanting to date me, not caring that I would likely not return for over a year, and resolved with her confession that when she kissed me, she was also cheating on her boyfriend, of at least ten years older than her. I did see him the first night, and she felt horrible that she wouldn't stop cheating on him. Politely, I told her I had to get to sleep, and not so politely, I told her to go away. I'd come to the realization that she was insane, a compulsive liar, and a horrible human. Cheating is not something I tolerate at all.

Waking up in a groggy daze, again I wasn't too sure about the events of the night before. My only evidence it had happened, were my texts from Molly or Polly, or whatever her real name might be. I hugged my family, thanked them immensely, and my Aunt gave me a reusable coffee cup for my travel. They helped me load my things in the car, and off I went.

Over Near Tennessee

After I left Annapolis, I had a long southbound drive ahead of me. My next place to stay was in Atlanta, and there's almost eighteen hours of driving between the two; I had some time to kill. Before my trip, people had told me repeatedly that I had to see Asheville, North Carolina. No one could really explain to me why I had to see it, but it was just important that I did. Interested, and headed that direction, my destination was set. I started driving that way, and realized I had nowhere to sleep once I arrived; for the first time, my car would be my home for over 24 hours.

I found myself on highways that were just main roads; the super highways of the North would be scattered from here on out. Once I'd gotten through Virginia, the cheaply priced cigarette capitol of the country, I finally entered North Carolina. Driving down their roads, I started to see mountains in the distance, specifically, the Blue Ridge Mountains. I had forgotten about them completely until I found myself looking up. I wanted badly to explore. It wasn't long before I also started seeing directional signs for the Blue Ridge Parkway.

Normally, when there are signs for a nearby attraction, it isn't too far off the road. The parkway's signs take you off the main road, onto a dirt road for about ten miles, and stop you at the base of the mountain; at least the route I went did. The base of the Blue Ridge Mountains, and the road that brings you up them, is very steep and winding. It also is the width of about one and a third cars. Climbing up, I knew two things: I could not turn around, and if someone came the opposite way, we would both die in a downhill slope.

Of course, I did manage to climb the mountainside and park my car. At the elevation, all communication with the outside world died, even the radio. The sun was shining and the wilderness was all around. Looking off the mountain sides, I could see well into several different states, most foreign to me. It was one of the most surreal moments of my life. I eventually moved my car to a different area, and realized that I was looking into Tennessee. The sun began to set and a light rain came down out of nowhere. Almost like an instinct, I played the Fleet Foxes out of my car, smoked a little of my weed, and watched the sun set into what would become one of my favorite states, though I didn't know it yet. If I could, I would relive that a million times over.

****

Once I left the mountains, I drove a couple more hours, and parked just outside Asheville in a rest stop on the side of the highway. It was in places like this that I would find myself sleeping often on my trip. I had been constantly advised that these were places where "gay people go to fuck." More than that, it was something I was told to be careful of, as if someone was going to show up and have sex with everyone. This sounded insane to me. As I hoped, I never had any run-ins with that unusual problem. Much like this night, most of the time I slept in these spots, it was from two, three, or four in the morning until sunrise, which would wake me and send me on my way.

This North Carolina rest stop, being my first on the trip, was also the first one to re-introduce me to the wonders that are coffee vending machines. As a child, my local bowling alley had one of these in its snack/vending machine room. I had not seen one in many years, and considering that the coffee is insanely cheap, it's really good coffee. Never consistent on price, but always between twenty-six and seventy-five cents, the machine pops out a styrofoam cup, and slowly but surely fills it with piping hot coffee to the brim. These machines take all coins as well because usually the price was something strange, like thirty-three, fifty-one, or sixty-seven cents, never something normal, like fifty. There are two major downsides to these machines; the first being the coffee is so hot you have to wait at least ten minutes before drinking it. The other is that there are never any covers for your cup, so you have to carefully walk away, spilling molten liquid everywhere you go, and hope it doesn't fall on your skin. Also, unless you're very skilled, a person can't buy a cup and then drive. I always loved the hot cup of coffee and the cool morning breeze as the sun came all the way up, before leaving the lot for my next destination.

Once I was walking around Asheville, I realized immediately why people like me, travelers, need to visit the town if they're near it. Asheville is a very relaxed town, and truly like a world of its own. It gives off the feeling of a college town, except there is no college around. The shops downtown are quaint and filled with just about anything you could want for fun. Pipes for smoking, old books for collecting, and great coffee for drinking, you'll find it there. Much like a miniature Denver, nearly everyone on the street has a smile on their face. I never saw anyone look twice at anyone during my time there.

It was still fairly early in the day but I can always go for a cup of coffee, so I wandered into a quiet, brick coffee shop. It was one of those shops where everyone who wasn't eating with their drink was reading a book or a newspaper. I got there at a good time, because there was only one person ahead of me in line.

"Oh! Hey Lexi," I could hear the barista say to the woman, "What would you like today?" I'm not sure what she ordered, but the man was happy to see her and got her food quickly. This warmed my heart, and it surprised me, as I've heard so many negative connotations toward the South; I was thrilled to see someone be so kind and nonjudgmental toward someone who is transsexual.

I remembered being at home, in Massachusetts, and watching my transsexual, transgender, and crossdressing friends and acquaintances experience great difficulty in the outside world. Not always, but often, they are asked to explain themselves to people. There's the awkward question, "What do we call you?" or God forbid, the alternative where people automatically use the incorrect pronoun and call someone "him" when they identify as "her." To make it easier, the English language has offered the gender-neutral term "they," if you are unsure.

Transgender and transsexual people alike are a very simple concept to grasp; they are people who identify as the opposite gender they were born. For those people who can't seem to grasp this, imagine yourself in a situation you've surely been in where you would rather not be. Now imagine that situation is with your physical being and the body you inhabit. Most people have had to live in a place they cannot comfortably call home, it's like that. With that simple explanation, I am appalled when someone says something along the lines of "I don't believe the trans *thing;* they just have a mental problem," or even worse when someone uses the English language's ugly cousin to "they," "it."

I've seen every kind of reaction to someone explaining they're trans, or to a trans person walking into an establishment, or even to me explaining what being trans means to someone. That being said, I was very happy to see the front man address Lexi with such joy. It also explains why I was so discouraged very quickly afterwards. I was enjoying a great cup of blueberry coffee with a bagel when a line started to form, almost out the door. I was fortunate to beat the rush, I suppose, but while sipping on a coffee to remember, I watched a man start to yell,

"Someone call the police! She's beating him!"

Everyone seemed confused, we couldn't see anything. He said it a few more times, and then we watched the woman, who had ordered her coffee just before me, run away from outside the shop. A shorter man, maybe in his forties, stood just off of the sidewalk, blood dripping from his face. When the police eventually showed up, they questioned the people nearby on the street, the bloody man, the man who called them, and the store clerk. From the beaten man, I learned that not only is he autistic, but she beat him for touching her bike; which is strange, because she ran away, leaving it still chained to the rack in front of the store. When the cop asked the clerk who the woman was, he replied,

"Lexi." The cop looked confused, so the clerk added, "The transgender girl; she comes in here almost every day!" He then knew exactly who she was and left the store.

Violence happens everywhere in this country, so I don't let that smudge the picture of Asheville I'd already seen. Instead, I enjoy the story for its hidden message; Lexi, although very angry for reasons I will never know, was only mentioned as transgender to the policeman because it helped explain who she was. It was as if the clerk had said, "You know, the girl with blue eyes," or, "The blonde, tall girl who's downtown a lot." It was not seen as a bad attribute of who she was, nor was she looked down upon, as she, unfortunately, might be in much of the country. This was the first but certainly not the final time I saw this kind of acceptance in the southern half of this country. I finished my coffee and food quickly; I was due in Atlanta that night.

Andy in Atlanta

As I was leaving Asheville, I texted my first Couchsurfing host, Andrea, to confirm our agreement that I was still to arrive at six that evening. She said that would be fine, but what she followed up with surprised me. "I live in a gated apartment complex. I will give you my code to get in, but DO NOT mention that you are from Couchsurfing to ANYONE AT ALL. If anyone asks who you are or where you're from, lie and say you're my friend visiting for the night."

Up to this point, she and I had been having very pleasant conversations about each other and my staying the night at her place. She had been nothing shy of polite and mild-tempered. So needless to say, this message alarmed me more than a little bit. For an arrangement that had been explained to me as easygoing and from a woman who didn't really seem to think twice about letting me be a guest, I didn't expect this to be a problem at all, let alone an alarmingly important one to her. I quickly questioned her on this, to which she firmly replied,

"Listen, I have many great reviews on this site and I'm letting you stay with me for free. Don't worry about why it's so important. It just is. I'll see you at six."

****

When I pulled up to the apartment complex, I was faced with the gate I already knew to exist. She wasn't kidding about it being a gated community; there honestly wasn't another way in or out of the place. Not even on foot could you leave except through the gate. Every building was shaped the same, but unique from any other I've ever seen. They had two pillars of apartments, each three floors tall, connected by hallways and staircases that are inside the pillars but still outdoors. As I parked in front of her building, I texted Andy saying that I had arrived. She quickly replied with a message telling me that she had run out for a minute but would be home shortly. Although I thought I'd be the only visitor that night, I decided to walk up to the third floor and knock on her door, thinking, maybe she has roommates that could let me in.

Two girls, roughly my age, answered the door and from behind the chain lock, asked who I was.

"Oh! I'm Max. I'm staying here for the night."

"Yes, but where did you come from. Who ARE you?"

"Sorry! I'm staying with Andy through Couchsurfing, she told me to meet her at this time."

After they opened the door for me, I was immediately in a small coatroom. To my right, I could go into the bathroom, or move forward into a living room area with a few mattresses and a TV. To the left was a closed door that belonged to Andy's room, and to the right were two more mattresses, one of which had a sleeping Brazilian woman in it. Beside her was a kitchen/ washroom. There was also a balcony outside, off the apartment facing the parking lot, opposite the room from Andy's door.

The short, blonde girl who let me in, Zoe, started talking to me. In her hair style and her general appearance, she looked like a pixie. The brunette, however, did not have time to tell me her name before she left. Zoe informed me that it was the girl's 21st birthday; she vanished into the Atlanta night and I would never see her again. The sleeping woman had just been broken up with and had been sleeping all day to cope. Zoe had a British accent and was the least materialistic person I had ever met. I watched her toss some pants and towels because they didn't fit in the suitcase any longer as well as leave a book behind because she had finished it and had no use for it. She also travels like I do, by saving like a bastard before leaving. She left England, alone, and traveled through Australia, New Zealand, and the Hawaiian Islands before making her way west to east across the continental states. The few empty beds in the living room were explained to me as being for people who weren't there at the time, but were all filled by morning. Zoe had an early morning train to catch for New Orleans.

She told me in a very hushed tone that, "We're not sure, but we think Andy might be transsexual."

I thought to myself that this would be great! Transsexual people are always interesting and usually good people. I mentioned that I know several, and met a transsexual woman at an untimely event in Asheville. I'd later learn, that although she is absolutely transsexual, it is also quite possibly the least interesting characteristic of Andrea. I also learned that she was not out running errands, but had to catch a poker game; I guess she's a big gambler.

When Andy finally did make it back to the apartment, she shook my hand and asked me to help her move a mattress out of her bedroom and into the living room for me to sleep on. She was a very aggressive woman.

"Did you mention Couchsurfing to anyone?"

"Well only to the two girls who let me inside earlier; they needed to know I wasn't a total stranger." I had thought her instruction was to not tell any guards or any janitors about

Couchsurfing; she should have been more blunt with me.

"Why would you do that?! Everyone else here is staying through Airbnb and are paying me thirty-five dollars per night! I'm doing you a favor, but if they ask, you are also paying me tonight." No one ever cared I was there for free, and she never asked me about paying.

After we moved my mattress for the night, she told me that a friend was coming over and they were going to be in her room for most of the night. If I absolutely needed anything I could interrupt, but she would rather not be bothered. Once her friend arrived, I would only see Andy for maybe forty-five scattered minutes ever again. Zoe and I exchanged traveling stories and tossed around the idea of me driving her to the train station in the morning.

As we kept talking, I watched a Brazilian man walk around, another go on the balcony and smoke a cigarette, and a woman fumble through the refrigerator. Before another could emerge, I decided to investigate and asked Zoe to hold on for a minute. Quickly, I learned that although upon entering the apartment your options are the bathroom and living room, there is a sort of third, hidden, option. Inside the bathroom is a door that to the naked eye looks like a closet. In actuality, behind this door is a huge open room with too many mattresses to count, back to back. There were about twenty-five to thirty Brazilians sleeping in there. There was also no other way into this hidden room. After asking Zoe, I learned that they were all staying for two months. With that information, I gathered that Andrea was making $875 per day and roughly $52,500 by the end of their visit; she also led me to believe she had a full time job. I knew some shady business was going on, and I did not want to wake up being the only other fluent English speaking person that morning. I told Zoe I would absolutely drive her.

****

In the morning, Zoe and I drove to the station and talked more about our ventures and the hope that we would eventually cross paths again. Once at the station, we learned her train was delayed and she began to complain about not having another book to read on the trip. Knowing damn well that its fate was to be left on that train seat beside Zoe, I gave her my beater copy of David Sedaris' "Me Talk Pretty One Day," because I thought it might make her laugh. It would possibly also end up in the hands of another train user or worker, who might enjoy it as much as I have. When her train came, we hugged and I waved her off. Then I drove into downtown, had the best grits I've ever eaten for breakfast and then explored the Coca-Cola museum, on a recommendation from Zoe.

****

Months later, after my trip finished, I received an email from Andy through Couchsurfing. In it she thanked me for my review of her, and asked if I could give the same review on her "actual" account, the one she usually uses. Because I had been working a lot, it took me a couple weeks to get to this. By the time I did, and had clicked on her link to the account, Couchsurfing informed me that "this user does not exist." Neither did her account that

I contacted her through. Although I stayed with Andrea in Atlanta, the other account claimed she lived in Montreal; or so said her email.

Looking back at it, aside from a box television, soap, and at least thirty-five mattresses, nothing else in her apartment had likely been purchased, but rather came with it. It had no photos on the walls or cabinets or anything of sentimental value. I suspect her name is not Andrea, she never lived in Atlanta full time, and she may be in court now.

Fair Enough

Although Andy was the first Couchsurfer I stayed with, Myron, from Milledgeville, Georgia, was the first I got in contact with. He understood that I didn't have any references yet and wanted nothing more than to help me. He even bought my comedy album, which few people would ever end up doing. Although a bit out of my way, I couldn't not go! I knew from his profile that he was from somewhere in South America, and seemed to be well educated. His profile didn't show much more, and so I began to ask questions like, "What do you do for work," "How long have you been a host," and even, "How old are you?" All of which were replied with, "Well haven't you Googled me, bro?!"

I had never considered Googling surfers, although, it might have been a good idea. It seemed off-putting and egotistical that someone would assume that I'd research them before meeting them though.

Myron added, "We can talk about stuff over dinner and a beer when you get here. I'll teach you about me and you teach me about comedy and how that works. I'm listening to your material right now, bro, it's hilarious." Myron's texting tone was not unlike foreigners who believe, in America, terms like bro, dude, and others are necessary to end nearly every statement. At a certain point in our texting, he must have gotten to the point in my album where I talk about getting too drunk with friends, specifically the part where I'm found naked hugging a toilet for no reason. He would then text me something to the effect of, "Woah man! No booze for you. I can't do that to you, bro!"

Not that I was hankering for alcohol, but I had an argument to make, "I can drink a beer, man, it's just part of a bit. It doesn't really matter to me though."

"No bro, no beer for this guy! Do you want apple or cranberry juice?"

"Wait, what? Why?"

"You've got to drink something, bro, right?"

Before I could respond with a juice flavor, he texted me, "I got it, bro. I just bought five gallons of prune juice for you!"

To this day, I don't know why he said that, not just the prune juice, any of it. It was a very strange conversation, that just got even weirder. He said something to me along the lines of, "I won't be home until five or so, can you meet then?" I replied with, "Sure, that sounds fair enough," which sent him into a tirade of text messages of why that was absolutely not fair enough, and what fair enough things are. An abridged version of what he said goes something like this,

"Fair enough?! No, it is not! Bro! I'll tell you what's fair enough; traveling on foot for weeks and finally seeing a bed is fair enough. Finding out who your parents are after you're already an adult is fair enough. Being homeless and needing a sink to shower before a meeting is fair enough. And being a vegetarian and not having a meal for days before someone hands you a cheeseburger is fair enough. Me changing the time is just how it's going to go, bro."

To make things even stranger, when I asked for his address, he ended the message with, "....great luck in Atlanta and everywhere else you hit/slam with your humor! BIG HUG, - Myron." As a storyteller, I knew I had to meet this man in person.

****

When I pulled into the driveway of the residential home, I was greeted by a very tan and oily Hispanic man, Myron. He welcomed me inside with open arms, and as I had suspected, there never was any prune juice, or juice at all. I opted to take a shower after the drive, and Myron told me that while I was in there, he was going to run to the grocery store.

After he left, I realized that he lived in a beautiful home; there were three bedrooms, a kitchen and living room, all professionally furnished and well decorated. Things were in boxes, I couldn't tell if he was moving in or out. Oddly not boxed up, were Myron's three framed bindings for the books he wrote in Spanish. When I later asked about them, I learned that Myron was a professor of Female Latin-

American Studies. I then took a shower in the bathroom connected to the spare room. When I was out and dressed, I was confused to be greeted by a taller burly man.

I asked, "Who are you?"

"Well, I'm Alec, who are you?"

"Max, I met Myron on Couchsurfing."

"Oh! He always does that. I had no idea we were expecting a guest. I'm his part time roommate. Ideally, I'd live with my wife, but work is much closer to here, so I live with Myron on some week nights. I have a desk job around here that I really hate. My passion lies in corsets."

Myron waked through the front door at this point and said, "How do steaks sound for dinner, guys? I was in the mood."

We both said sure, and Alec went on a bit further, "So I've always liked them, but never saw it as more than a hobby. I own many of them, but again, it was a hobby. Then I started talking to a coworker at my desk job about them, and we looked into going into business together. It was quite an investment, but on our seven year plan, we're ahead of schedule on sales. I ran it by my wife too, and the three of us work together on them. Unfortunately, it's not at the point where any of us can live off our sales. For now most of the money goes back into the company."

"Wow man! That's awesome, but is there a market for them big enough to support a company?"

"Yeah! They're making a comeback like vinyl records. Cosplayers, role-players, men and women trying to look better for their partners and transsexuals use them all the time. My gimmick is selling them closer to the price the factory gives me, and undercutting the bigger businesses. They can sell a similar corset for two hundred and fifty dollars, and mine will cost seventy-five. They're similar styles, and similar results, but cheaper prices. And those who use them often for the better body shape, have to keep buying newer ones to fit their new bodies. It works really well for us; we all wear them too. Well not Myron, but most of my friends do."

Myron rolled his eyes and giggled. "Dinner's ready, let's eat and talk about something else."

Once at the dinner table, I asked the two of them, "So I saw all the boxes, are you guys moving in or packing up to leave?"

Myron answered, "Leaving, actually. Our other roommate moved out already, and that's actually the room you'll be staying in. I'm headed back out to San Diego to live near my family."

Alec jumped in, "Yeah and I got a deal on a boat house nearby, too. We're leaving in a few days actually, you're probably the last visitor we'll have here."

"Wow, thank you so much for hosting me so close to the move!"

"Myron just loves meeting new people man," Alec chuckled, "I do too, but it is in the end of our stay here."

"Well thank you for the dinner, it's wonderful!"

"No problem, the least I can do is feed guests," Myron smiled, and motioned us to the living room, where Alec quickly went back to his talk of work. "They're not bad for you like most people think. If worn correctly, they're quite healthy and reshape your figure to be more attractive to people. We go to conventions for these all the time, and often they're anime conventions. It's pretty great to be able to touch beautiful women's bodies in my work."

Myron smile and chuckled to himself, "Show him the magazine."

"You sure? My magazine? The one you know is always with me?"

"Yeah sure, who cares!"

As he got up, I looked at grinning Myron, and shrugged my shoulders, "Just wait," he said.

Alec returned with a 2002 Playboy issue, with a very tattooed woman wearing a corset on the front. "She's my idol," he told me, "Sure she's naked here, but look at her body! That's from a corset. That's how I want my clients to look and feel about themselves, so confident! I don't show many people this, they think it's weird I carry an old nude magazine with me everywhere."

"Hey man, you use it for art, it's alright."

"Yeah, not always art," Myron laughed to himself.

"Well thanks for that Myron, but on that note, I have to leave around five in the morning, I'm headed to bed. It was nice meeting you, Max. Goodnight."

"Goodnight."

"Myron, you're moving to San Diego, could I crash with you when I'm out there? I'll need a place."

"Oh! You're actually doing the whole country! Well, if you bring two gallons of water, sure," he laughed again, "three, if you want a shower! But sure thing! I also have to get to bed, but I'll see you another time! Leave whenever you need, we won't wake you. I'm going to leave the coffee on for you, but please turn it off when you go. Alec and I will both be gone when you wake up, I think."

"Thank you for everything man, really. I appreciate it all!"

"Night!"

The Saggy State

After leaving Myron and Alec, I moved south, to meet another Couchsurfer, Kelly, in Tallahassee. I had never driven through Florida; the last time I was there I was four years old. I was blown away when I drove past my first palm tree. I fell in love with them, and the weather of the state. Elderly people retire to Florida, and I totally understand why. When I arrived at her house, Kelly answered the door with a smile. The woman was in her mid-twenties, very tan, and well fit. She also screamed everything she said, which was a little more than offsetting since she didn't know she was doing it.

"I'm just waiting for another guest to visit, his name is Jared and we're going to get dinner. You can come if you want. You'll be staying on the couch tonight, he booked staying with me on Couchsurfing before you did," she yelled all of this very matter-of-factly, almost as if she was punishing me with the information.

"Oh and this is Kitty, my sister's cat. I'm babysitting her, and I can't remember her name, so it's Kitty while she's here. Come here Kitty!"

"Alright, well when he gets here I'll make the call, but sure I can go to get food with you guys, I'm pretty hungry. So what do you do except for Couchsurf? Any hobbies or anything?"

"Well! I like going to the gym, and I'm an attorney in Florida, it's alright, I guess. I'm going to go for a run, make yourself at home, and I'll be back before Jared gets here!"

When she shut the door behind her, I started to make the living room my home for the night. I brought my suitcase inside, and started to play with Kitty. Looking around, I noticed the apartment was two floors tall, had two bathrooms, two bedrooms, a kitchen, and the living room. This room was a good size, but felt a little empty. It had a couch, a tv, a bookcase with about 500 dvds in it, and a coffee table. On the coffee table was a book with a title something along the lines of, "Your Birth Date, Your Ideal Sexual Positions, and More!" Sure,

Kelly is a good looking woman, but I was curious about how many guests had flipped through this awkward book. I did not want that answer.

After a short amount of time Kelly returned, and Jared arrived. Jared taught film classes in Boston; it was a neat coincidence that we would both Couchsurf from Massachusetts to Kelly's apartment. He's in his early thirties, very well groomed, and well spoken. We were talking about coming from the same area, when Kelly started trying to impress Jared from the other room.

"I told Max, but I'm an attorney in Florida and Georgia. I'm from there, Georgia, but I can also practice law in D.C. If you have your license in any state, you have it there too," I hadn't realized until this point how ditzy she was, "I just want to travel a bit more, you know? I wish I could practice in the state of Cuba."

When she said that, Jared and I looked at each other, and silently agreed to not correct her.

We went out for Mexican food that night, and afterwards watched one of Jared's favorite films, Michael Douglas' *The Game*, and shared a bottle of red wine. Kelly was a big drinker, and asked Jared to look for his birthday and sexual position correlation in her book. She wanted him badly, and he wanted no part in it. I have never felt badly about being a third wheel to her. While Jared and I shared conversations about travel and our lives over a glass, Kelly contributed little to the conversation and had the bottle. She mentioned she would be working by the time we left in the morning, and headed to bed. Before she did, I asked if she would mind if I returned on my departure from the state a couple weeks later. She said she didn't care, went to sleep, and shortly after so did both of us. The next morning, I woke after Jared and Kelly had left. I found a note near the couch from Jared, "Good talking last night. Hope to catch you back in Boston, have a great adventure." I smiled at the kind note, I gathered my belongings, and headed to my friend's house in Tampa.

****

I was staying with my childhood friend, Francesca and her roommate, in Tampa. Both women have a similar build; they look like they belong in an anime. They are both mid height, with very fit bodies and giant breasts. They lived together for the convenience of being near their school. After catching up for a little while, Francesca couldn't hold it in anymore, "I'm having a baby! Not many people know, but I had to say it! I'm going to be a mom!" I didn't even know if she was even dating anyone, so this was a huge surprise to me. "My boyfriend is named Brian, and we haven't been together very long. I told him he could leave and have no repercussions from me, but he didn't and we're both excited! He's a state cop down here and we're looking at getting a house or apartment together after my lease here runs out. It's scary but wonderful!"

"Woah! Congratulations! That's huge news, I'm so happy for you and can't wait to meet the guy!"

"He's actually coming over tomorrow to meet you. He didn't really get why I was helping you out. We've never been really close, but it's what you do with a friend from back home. Apparently, it's not a thing that happens if you're from Florida. I'm sorry to cut it short, but I have to get to work. Make yourself at home, stay as long as you need, and I'll see you later on." She handed me a house key and left.

I then got high with her roommate, who told me all about going to school for fashion, her plans to maybe move to California after Francesca moves in with Brian, and the struggle of paying for rent. I told her about my comedy, and asked if she knew of any open mics in the area. She didn't and then took a phone call, and walked away. I took that time to look for an open mic for that night. I found several in the area, but decided on a place called "The Witch's Brew" in Palm Harbor.

****

The Witch's Brew is a coffee shop/ beer and wine bar/ hot dog stand/ thrift shop/ marijuana petition site. I think the woman who owns it put all of her favorite things in a small shop and hoped for the best. It is also a very cool outdoor venue with ashtrays everywhere. I was smoking a cigarette while finalizing my set for the night, which was supposed to be about ten minutes, and watching the act before me play their music. The band was all elderly people playing hillbilly music, with washboards, banjos, and flutes.

They were wonderfully talented, and I've never seen anything like it before. The group played several of their own pieces as well as popular songs rewritten for their style, such as early Beatles music.

When it was finally my turn, I told my stories and was edged on further by the crowd. Several people were really into my set, and I ended up going for over a half hour. The owner was into my material and signaled me to keep going. When I went back to take my seat, an older man with droopy eyes and relaxed clothing tapped me on the back. I turned, and he promptly fell back, out of his chair, and spilled wine everywhere.

"Are you okay man? I'm sorry you spilled that everywhere."

"Don't worry about that. I'm fine, but I want to talk with you. Take a seat?" I sat down beside him.

"I like your stuff; you're good, but I was watching the audience as well as you. I was engaged in all your stories, but everyone else was into a handful each," he pointed people out in front of us, "You need to be able to hook them for the whole time. You need to jab them harder with each story; make them want you more. Do you know who I am?"

I assumed I was talking with a drunk guy who didn't know what he was talking about, or maybe even where he was.
"No, I don't. Should I?"

He smiled, "I'm John Hobbs. It's okay if you don't know me, but I can help you. I worked closely with Meir Ezra for years and after that ended, I pursued other investments, like the workout gear I invented." He went to show me photos of a prototype of his. It's a weighted water bottle that's strapped to wrist bands for runners. They come in sets of two and are available now. The purpose is for runners to not run out of water as quickly, and the weights work out your arms as you run, and make the water seem easier to carry. "I help out a lot here financially, and know all about talking publicly. I started out shaky like you, then Meir helped me and so did a couple organizations." He seemed to totally sober up by this point.

"Wow! I had no idea, I'd love to keep talking. I'm all ears on what you can offer me." John went on to suggest business techniques to further my career, direct me to people who could help me, and an organization to help me speak better publicly. Our conversation would last well over an hour, and I realized I was due back at Francesca's apartment. I told John I had to leave, and gave him a copy of my CD. Perhaps he knew what to do with it.

****

The next day, my last day in town, I met Brian, Francesca's boyfriend. He was a very proud police officer, who worked his ass off. My mother had told me something that I planned to work into my stand up after leaving Florida, and I had to tell Brian.

"Hey man, before I left my mother was talking to someone from Florida on the phone. Afterwards she pulled me aside, and I think you'll like what she had to say."

"Alright, man, what happened?" He seemed to not believe I had a story for him, almost brushed it off.

"She came up to me and said, 'Max, you need to be careful in Florida, the cops there are dangerous. I'm just worried. They're down there molesting everybody, all the time. It's getting insane!'

Mom, no they're not. It would be on the news!

Look, I don't know how they get away with it, but it's happening all the time.

Like mid-day, whenever?

I guess so! Look I want you to be prepared. It's not like you have to watch out, it's just going to happen. It's okay down there somehow!

No, it isn't! But sure, I'll watch out.'"

Brian was fixed on that and thought to himself for a moment, then asked, "I'm sorry, what?"

"Yeah, I hope you guys don't do that here, but know that it's horribly socially acceptable in my mother's weird view of the world."

"I've never heard of such a thing happening ever! I could never!"

I turned to a laughing Francesca, "Well, he's got that going for you!"

We ate dinner together, and shared stories for most of the night, until the next morning, when I headed further south to meet up with family in Port Charlotte.

Still Sagging

I was staying with my cousin, Rachel, her boyfriend, and her daughter in Port Charlotte. While there, her boyfriend, Colin, took a day off work to spend the day with me, to show me the things he enjoys in the area. I told him that was a great idea, but before we did anything, I had to find a few boxes to ship things back north. I had a few birthday gifts that were already late. He insisted upon buying boxes at the post office to ship my things, and I kept asking if a local grocery store or Walmart might toss some away for customers to take. He looked at me with confusion and disbelief. He took me to several post offices or UPS stores, before I shut him up and asked someone on the street if they knew a place that got rid of boxes for free. We were directed to a nearby Subway, and I found some there. It was as if this man had never mailed anything before. Doing it his way would've cost me about ten dollars more.

Once the mail had shipped, he explained that he really wanted to show me his favorite local indoor gun range as well as go canoeing. I'd done neither of these things before, and he knew that. We went to the shooting range first, and he brought out his gun and hung up a target for me to use. After a sped up tutorial on gun safety and use, he handed me the firearm, told me to square my shoulders, and see how I did. Colin tells the story best, and his version goes like this,

"I don't really know what happened. Max's shoulders were square, he was holding it right, the aim looked good, and then, I don't know. He just kinda missed."

What I had actually done, was miss the target completely and hit the closeline that hangs it, completely destroying the mechanism. It looked like my bullet initially hit the clamp holding the target, and ricocheted up, into the wire itself. The whole contraption fell to the ground, and after alerting an employee, we were told to keep going. Not only that, but the man running the store told us not to worry about the damage! I offered to pay to have the line fixed, but he just walked away, muttering, "I just fixed it yesterday!" We moved to the closeline beside us, and for some reason, Colin decided to hand me the gun again, to have another go at it. I did better, and actually hit the piece of paper a few times, but I probably shouldn't have ever been handed a gun again after the first shot.

Later on, we went to a dock and rented a canoe. After telling him over and over that this was yet another thing I had never done, he decided to have us canoe in a river infested with alligators and manatees. Another risky idea, but I went along. Had we tipped over, we may have died, and he and the man we rented from made damn sure I knew that. I learned quickly that in a canoe built for two, the front person steers while the rear works as an engine and sends us forward. Colin put me in front, claiming that, "it'll be easier for you," and it would have been, had he not forgotten to put any force into his half of the vessel. I like Colin a lot, but he's full of bad ideas that always somehow work out. We never tipped over, or even saw an alligator, but we did see some manatees swimming below us, and we did crash into a couple trees during the venture.

We had lost track of time, so once we finally docked we were already late for picking up Rachel from work. We rushed to her, then immediately picked up her daughter from school. They decided to treat me to dinner at an alligator themed restaurant. I was curious, sure, but more than that, I was cautious to eat an animal that I didn't know anyone ate, let alone base an entire restaurant on. I felt like a fancy version of what the first guy to eat oysters must've felt like. Alligator is an animal that makes me wonder who might have been first to say, "Let's eat it!" It's like if chicken and shrimp had a gummy baby. Once I did eat my alligator cheesesteak, I fell in love with the meat. Surprisingly, it is one of the best tasting meats, maybe second only to venison, from what I've tried. I can't recommend it enough!

****

While in the area, I visited a family friend of my parents, but I didn't meet him until I was nineteen, so he's just another guy to me. He's a very tall, white, balding, and muscular man. His name is Paul and he is possibly the most racist man I've ever met. If you aren't Caucasian, he immediately has a problem with you. Weirdly, other minorities, such as homosexuals or the disabled, don't bother him in the slightest. I somehow was able to look past his racist nature for the night, and he and I talked all night about my family and our lives in the nearly twenty years before we met. We shared a lot of laughs, and then I asked him to look over my car. He's no mechanic, but he knows what he's looking at and can lend a hand if needed.

"Well, Max, it runs fine, right? Everything looks good, but your AC is shot. You won't have that until you take it to a shop or something. If I had a couple days, I'd be able to help you out, but I don't."

"Well thanks for looking and letting me know how it is."

"Yeah of course, I know you gotta get going soon, but let me know how it all goes. I'll see you when I see you!"

"Take care, Paul."

He went into his home, and I went off to go ten-pin bowling with my cousin. This was yet another thing I had never done; having grown up in New England, Massachusetts only has candlepin bowling, which for those who don't know the difference, the rules are the same, but ten-pin is big ball bowling, and candlepin is little. After bowling a few strings, we hugged, and said farewell. This was the last time I would see family, or anything close to it, until I arrived in Phoenix.

****

On my way out of Florida I stayed with Kelly once again, and she told me, in her deafening voice, that more Couchsurfers would join us. They were from Spain and traveling the country as well. Their names were Dani and Macarena, a name that I would never tell her is hilarious to Americans because of the Los del Rio song. He is a tall, clean cut, tan man, and she is a shorter girl with the same descriptions. They're a beautiful couple.

They had been studying abroad in Canada and before heading home, wanted to see part of the United States. They were very outgoing, and on the first day we spent together, they invited me to go with them to a nearby Spanish-American history museum. Kelly opted to stay home, and off we went. The exhibits there were amazing, filled with information about the Native American war with the Spaniards. My companions knew far more of the information than I did, but we all had a great time. That night at Kelly's, I learned a lot about Spanish culture from them, which started when I asked them to play cards. They said sure, and when I took out a deck of Bicycle cards, they looked confused.

"What are these?"

"Cards, what do you mean?"

"We're used to our cards, I guess they're different. Our deck uses only 48 cards and not suit symbols like these, but a coin system."

Their English was near perfect, but they never explained the coin system; I gathered it was a color scheme or something like that. They taught me a trump based game much like a dumbed down pinochle. We removed the jacks from my deck and it worked well enough. I won each game; English games must be more complicated than Spanish, I guess. While playing, I learned more about their home.

"You know, in Spain we all speak Spanish, but there are different dialects, like Chinese. The country is divided in fourths, so, to correspond, someone in the northeast talking to someone from the southwest would only have a brief understanding of one another."

"Wow I had no idea! You guys have been together awhile, I'm guessing?"

"About seven years now, yeah."

"Are you married?"

I was a little confused when they both laughed at me, "No! No one hardly ever gets married in Spain, it's a rarity. If we were to tell our friends and family we were considering it they'd tell us we haven't been together long enough! Americans do it too fast, that's why so many divorces happen here! It's almost a fifty-fifty chance that a marriage will work here, right?"

"Yeah! That's such a culture shock to me though, I had no idea!"

"Yeah, so almost no one ever gets divorced," Dani went on, "I only know one couple to have split up after a marriage, and it was so strange no one knew how to handle it!"

"I can't even imagine that," I said.

****

The following day was our departure from Kelly and Tallahassee. We all said goodbye to her, and at the last minute, Dani and Macarena invited me to go with them to the Wakulla Springs, just north of Tallahassee! Of course I said yes, I enjoyed the two of them a lot, and there, we swam in clean water with manatees. The springs were shallow, and there was a rope to prevent people from swimming into dangerous currents. There was a long wooden walkway over the water for people to jump off of, and it was a beautiful, clear day until it started to rain as we left. We saw a mother manatee looking after two of her children, and had a great day of it. By the time we had to split up, we had become great friends. They kept, and continue to keep, telling me that I have to go to

Spain to see them. They say it as though it's a hop, skip, and a jump away.

A Very Proud Red Hippie

As I was leaving Florida, I found myself
driving through the worst rain storm of my life.
Nearly every car on the highway pulled over for
long lengths of time, and while driving, I
couldn't see the cars in front of or beside me. It
was so bad, that out of other options, I pulled
into a rest stop and told my next host, Ed, that I
would be late. Ed was a man I found on
Couchsurfing, and he told me that he didn't
even expect me at all, not because of the rain,
but because Couchsurfers often blow him off.
He begged off the conversation because he was
working, and with the rain sounding like it was
coming through the roof, I took a nap.

After enjoying a coffee from the vending
machine, I trenched back into the stormy
highway, and north to Wetumpka, Alabama.
The town borders Montgomery, in the north, but
is very remote. Ed's house is even more remote;
I wouldn't have found it if I didn't see his
streetside mailbox. The house is up on a steep
dirt hill with a narrow gravel driveway Once up

the hill, you can see a building that looks very old, surrounded by plants and half-finished wooden artistic projects. When he let me inside, I could see a very oddly furnished home. From old mismatched couches to odd art on the walls, and from a lack of a television to a bathroom filled with hung up clothes, this house was a different world altogether.

"Well," he would explain, "I don't really see why you wouldn't buy all furniture and fixtures at a thrift shop like the Salvation Army. I've bought most of the art that I have there, as well as the light switches, couches, rugs, and damn near everything else! And electricity is so damn expensive, so I only use it for what I need, like the refrigerator and washing machine. I have a drier, but only use it when I'm in a hurry or it's freezing outside and the hanger won't dry the clothes. It's almost never plugged in."

We started to make macaroni for dinner when he went on to ask me, "Wait, you're not a hippie are you? I hate hippies, they freeload and make a mess. I love Couchsurfers and all, but we contribute and make friends, don't just sleep a hangover off or whatever."

"No man, I'm not a hippie, I'm just a traveler and trying to figure life out."

"Good! Sure, I mean, I love going to concerts and getting stoned and maybe tripping a little, but I work a hard life. I'm responsible, that's the difference. I guess I'm kinda like a redneck, I drive my truck and like getting drunk." I've always thought his description of himself makes him sound like both a redneck and a hippie, but don't tell him that.

"I mean I get high too man; do you want some?"

"No thanks man, I work at five in the morning, but feel free to smoke wherever. Smoke in the living room if you'd like."

"You sure? Alright man; thanks for dinner by the way."

"Don't worry about it! Take some snacks when you leave in the morning, too. I'll have already left for work but help yourself to whatever you'd like. I saw you do comedy, want to try some out on me? I listen to NPR constantly and love spoken word. I'll let you know if you're any good or not."

I went on to tell him about four of my stories I tell to crowds often and he chuckled a little bit on them all.

He commentated, "You should be on The Moth, man," The Moth is a very popular storytelling program on NPR, "You're funny and tell those really well!"

"Wow, thanks Ed!"

We had moved to the living room around this time and sat down to continue talking,

"You know, people call me Ed and it's how I refer to myself often, but other people call me Kenny, or Kenneth. It's a little weird, but it's always been like that."

This Rocky Raccoon scenario was never explained to me further. I don't know which name is legally correct, but it makes me smile to this day.

"You know, the North sucks! I don't mean it racially, and I don't mean you, but you guys are ruining the South. Yeah sure we smoke weed and drive drunk a lot, and that's not good, don't get me wrong. But you guys have meth. Meth! I've never seen meth. Your state has a huge heroin problem, right? I bet your town even does. That's starting to come down here, until a few years ago, I had never seen heroin or heard of doing it! You only smoke weed right?"

"Yeah man, weed and cigarettes. But you're right, we have a huge drug problem up there. I never thought about the North and South differences like that."

"Well, good, I mean you should try acid sometime, but don't do anything else. It's killing fucking everyone! Goddamn, I hate the North for that reason! I don't care about the politics, and we, down here, are often too racist, sure, but fuck the drugs!"

This argument was the only one ever given to me about why the South is better than the North and it also makes a lot of sense. This country does have a massive drug problem, and although I couldn't speak for the whole North half of the nation, New England is filled with a massive problem. Ed hit it right on the money when he mentioned my town specifically having a problem. Haverhill, Massachusetts has an enormous heroin problem and is headline news almost every day.

"Well, I'm going to go to bed, make yourself comfortable on that couch and leave whenever you want in the morning. I'll be quiet leaving, and it's been great talking and I hope to see you again sometime! Goodnight!"

"Goodnight! Thank you so much!"

****

When I woke up, I smoked weed in his living room. I took some snacks, and left him a note that said thank you, and started my way to Nashville, Tennessee.

Pixie and the Pot

I used Ed's home as a rest point on my drive
from Florida up to Spring Hill, Tennessee.
There, I would meet up with my father's former
coworker, Erin. The two worked together in
newspapers some years ago; my dad also
worked with Erin's mother. Erin was part time
then and was now more than thrilled to house
me for as long as I needed. She lived in a row
home styled condominium complex. When I
arrived, a blonde woman, a little older than me,
was getting out of her car. This, I learned, was
Erin. She hugged me, and offered to bring my
things inside, where her cat immediately started
giving me the stink eye. She told me to make
myself at home, and showed me my room,
which was normally dedicated to her cat. See,
Erin lives alone, but her cat, Pixie, stands in as a
roommate, and arguably, a life partner. She's a
normal looking white cat, but she acts like
someone just gave her catnip, constantly. The
night I arrived, Erin and I decided to go out for

pizza at a really nice place and learn a bit about each other.

That night, I learned a lot. She started out with, "Well, my dad died a little while ago, and I didn't know it, but he had a small fortune. I inherited all of it and haven't really worked in a while because of it. I just live with my kitty and watch TV most of the time. It's nice. I mean I should get something going, but it's like a permanent vacation. With his money, I bought the place I live in without a mortgage, just cash in hand really."

"Wow! I'm so sorry, but congrats. That's a huge accomplishment, buying a home so early on without debt."

"Yeah, I used to live a couple towns over with my mom, but decided to get away a little."

"Why'd you guys move down here from Mass anyway?"

"We were tired of it, and basically pointed to a random place on a map and went. We've lived here ever since. I like it a lot."

Somewhere around this time, our food came to us, and she continued, "Well I actually did just start selling Dove Chocolates. You know, like people sell Avon stuff, with parties and things."

"Yeah, my mom used to do that. How's it going?"

"I haven't really started yet but I've been leaving my books for it everywhere, the hair dresser's, grocery store, even here there are some! But anyways, your dad said you might be looking for open mics down here?"

"Yeah if you know of any that'd help a lot!"

"There's a ton of them around; check out Nashville if you want. It's like a half hour from my house. I'm sure you'll find something."

"Thanks! I'll go up there tomorrow I guess."

"Oh right," she reached into her pocket and handed me a key, "Take this for while you're here. I won't be home much because of the guy I'm kind of seeing. Well not really, I don't know. We've been sleeping together for about three years now, and go on dates and stuff, but we're not boyfriend and girlfriend. He wants it like that; it's good, you know? I really like it this way, sometime we'll talk every day, and other times we won't speak for a few weeks. But the dynamic never changes." She said this very matter of factly, and almost like she was talking to herself.

"I'm sorry? That doesn't sound ideal to me, but it sounds like it kind of works. So congrats?"

"No, I'm serious. I like it a lot. He's the best. I'll be at his place for a lot of your stay, I hope that's okay."

"Yeah sure, no worries there!"

"Oh wow! It's gotten late and we should head back soon so you can sleep, huh? You must be tired from the driving, right?"

"Yeah, you're right I could use some sleep."

Erin's situation seemed bleak to me at the time, but since this conversation, she has gotten engaged and lives with that man. I guess I didn't know what I was talking about.

****

The next morning, when I woke up, Erin had already left for her day's errands. Emily, from back home, had said she found an open mic for me to play in Nashville that night, and so I decided to make some food and head to the city early to check it out. When I opened my door, I was greeted with an angry Pixie, who's litter box was still in her, I mean my, room. I suppose she was well trained, and waited until I woke up to go, but she looked at me until I left, with a stare that said, "I fucking hate you."

After I left Erin's home, her elderly neighbor greeted me by my car. She introduced herself to me as Edna. She must have been eighty, and surely shorter than five feet. "I saw your Massachusetts plates and wondered who you could possibly be!"

"Well, I'm taking a road trip across the country, and Erin was kind enough to have me stay a few days, I'm Max by the way."

"Well hello Max! That's wonderful. I used to live up there myself, until my son moved me down here, then left again. I told him, that's it. I'm not moving again, this is my last home, so help me God."

I opened my car door to leave, and she went on, "It's so brave of you to be doing this, I'll let you get going, but I hope to talk to you soon before you leave!"

"Alright, Edna, I'll make sure of it!" I closed my door, backed out, and she waved me off. She's an old lonely lady, and I wished I could've talked to her more.

Once I'd parked downtown, I immediately fell in love with the culture of the city. Nashville is set up like New York, and has a numbered grid system for the major roads. On first through fourth streets, every fifty feet or so, there's a different musical street performer. Most people associate Nashville with country music, but the performers play all kinds of music and most are wonderfully talented. At one point, I watched a six piece, acoustic, stringed arrangement play pop songs together, and as quickly as they came, they went. The acts don't last too long. Right down the street, were two men rapping, also very well. At the end of the road was a woman fronting a country cover group, and to the ear, she might as well have been Carrie Underwood.

That night I walked into the open mic Emily had set up, however, she'd failed to mention that it was a bar. For the only time in my underage career, I lied and said I was twenty-two years old. No one questioned me further. It was a comedy exclusive night; we each got four minutes, and the bar was one you can only find in the south. They had ash trays at every booth, table, or counter. There was even one on stage; for a smoker, this might as well have been France! When it was my turn, I told a couple of my stories, and got a terrific response. After the show had ended, the comedians milled around talking to one another, and I found myself talking to the night's host, Sean Parrott. His name sounds like either a cheap mixed drink, or a weird kind of sex. He asked all about my travels and of Boston. Then he pulled out his phone.

"This! You've got to go to this! Hold on, umm, do you have Facebook? I'll send it to you there!"

"What is it man?"

"This!" He showed me an event page for a house party that was also an open mic, "You'll do great here! A few of the people from tonight are going too!"

"Sure, but I don't know the woman who's house this is at."

"It doesn't matter, just go! I'll be there, I'll say we know each other! It'll be fun!"

I never saw Sean Parrott again, but I did go to the party. There, I met many wonderful people, such as a woman named Stephanie who was passing out business cards that only had her name and email on them. She called them something like "getting to know me cards." I liked the idea of that. I also met two men named Josh and Brett, also comedians, and the two showed me how welcoming and accepting the underground comedy scene of Nashville really can be. They provided me with some friendly advice on how I could get more laughs out of one of my stories, and Brett even invited me to other open mics during my stay out there. After we'd all gone outside to smoke cigarettes, Josh and another guy invited us to their apartment, down the road. Our hostess needed sleep.

At Josh's, we started talking more about our lives as comedians. Someone said, "Something something getting stoned," so I brought in my weed from the car, which they topped off and we spent most of the night stoned and talking about foreign films. For a rare moment, I felt I had found my people.

****

The next morning, in Erin's kitchen, I started looking for a way to make coffee. It wasn't until she told me she hadn't had a cup in years, that I engineered a new way to do it. I took a folded paper towel, and placed it just over my cup, put grounds in there, and slowly poured boiling water over it. I would get an alright cup about every four out of five times. I noticed that about a lot of the country, most of the south doesn't drink coffee. This paper towel trick would be used many more times throughout my trip.

On my last day in Tennessee, I walked around Nashville one more time, and eventually, sat down on a bench by a fountain. For the only time during this trip, I seriously considered moving there and ending my journey. I even did minor apartment hunting. Sometimes I wonder what might have been, but I knew I had to finish the trip and come back later on. My grandfather called me too, to tell me that he'd listened to my album through a few times, and liked that I was doing comedy, but said, "it needs a lot of work."

Before leaving all together, I'd packed all of my things in my car, and Edna came back outside. She handed me an envelope and closed it in my hands. "Don't open it until I've gone inside, but in there is my address. I want you to mail me a postcard after your trips finished. I want to hear back from you, promise me you'll send it?"

"Of course I will!" I smiled.

"Well good, drive safe now."

The envelope contained forty dollars, a letter, with her address, and other things like tissues that she thought I could use. She's a very sweet lady and I did send her a postcard.

Turn Around!

During my twelve years of public education, my history courses all spent a great deal of time on the Civil Rights Movement. Although we watched Martin Luther King's speeches, read excerpts of Malcolm X's autobiography, and read the newspaper clippings from when Rosa Parks became an icon, far and away, I remember spending the most amount of time on the children who were the Little Rock Nine.

These nine children were made famous because of the result of the Brown vs The Board of Education ruling. This supreme court case desegregated schools, and in Little Rock, Arkansas, nine African American children began attending a formally Caucasian school. They were tormented, beaten, and suffered a lifetime's worth of abuse in only a few months. Although their lives at the time weren't ideal, they helped pave the way for integrated schools all across America, and I wanted to see the school where it all happened.

****

While in Spring Hill, I began exchanging messages on Couchsurfing with a man named Daven, short for Davenport, like the town. He seemed to be a mid-twenties, easygoing guy and eventually we exchanged phone numbers. I don't know what he did for work, but it was flexible and he could begin his workday at really any time. He was also very apologetic toward me because he double booked me with a couple from Connecticut. I was truly happy to hear this, because I enjoyed meeting new travelers, and usually, I prefer them to my hosts. At this point, I knew nothing more about the couple other than their existence.

I planned to arrive on a Sunday evening, and told Daven to expect me around 9PM. After leaving Memphis, I was faced with awful road traffic and when, at 7:30, Daven called me to ask if I was arriving at 9 still, I told him,

"I think it's going to be closer to 9:30, if that's alright."

He replied in a very slow, somber, and bobbing voice, almost nervously, "Yeah, yeah, yeah, that'll be fine. Hey, I'm so sorry, I double booked, I forgot about both, of you guys, and no one, ever shows up, from Couchsurfing."

"I'm sure it'll be alright man, hosts double or even triple book guests all the time."

"Yeah, well, Max, we were, thinking, maybe, if you're not too tired, I don't know, would you, maybe, want to, go to, the movies, with us, tonight?"

While in reality, I was very tired and had no real interest in seeing a film, I said, "Sure…" because this man was letting me stay with him for free. The least I could do was go see a movie with him, I'd even pay if asked.

"Well what, do you think, you might, want to see?" asked Daven

"I haven't really seen much T.V. in the past month or so, so I don't really know what's playing now. I'm sure whatever you guys want to see will be wonderful."

"Well, have you, seen Mad Max, Fury Road?"

"No, I haven't, have you? That sounds good to me."

Daven's voice would change two times in our knowing each other; this was the first. His tone was no longer somber, or anything near it, but rather like daggers, possibly on crack.

"Yeah! I've seen it! It's Fucking awesome! It's Gonna be, a Fucking, awesome night! I can't, Fucking wait! Yeah! It's Fucking Awesome!"

Every time he said "Fucking" the word always ended with a hard "G" sound.

"Well alright man! Is there a showing around 9:30 though?"

"Yeah! It's actually, at 9:30, but you can miss the first ten minutes or so, I'll catch you up, They're not really important."

This, about the first ten minutes, was simply a lie.

He continued, "So where are you now!?"

Although, I cannot recall it now, I read to him the name of the town that my upcoming highway sign read.

` "You'll, be here, before 9:30! That's like, ten minutes, from my house! You're way closer!"

I'm certain Daven has a much better understanding of Arkansas towns and cities than I do, however, my directions showed me having at least ninety minutes left of my drive. I also may have been speaking condescendingly at this, largely because Daven's tone of voice was nothing short of offsetting at this point, "Well, my GPS says it'll be an hour and a half at least, I'm not going to stop driving, and I'll call you when I arrive, we will see how long it takes."

"Yeah. I guess, we Will see!"

I suppose I wouldn't have believed me either if I knew the towns, and there could have been a quicker route to get to his house, but this was the easiest most direct way I could find. And on a road trip, alone, in a totally strange place, that's exactly what I wanted.

"So I'll call you when I get there?"

"Yeah, that sounds fine, I'll talk to you later."

"Talk to you soon man,"

The phone call ended.

****

Sure enough, I pulled into his apartment complex at 9:30 that night. Although it is an apartment, the buildings look more like row homes, all two floors tall, and each sharing walls with their neighbors. The complex also has a pool and tennis courts for the community.

"Hey man, I'm at your place, could you let me in?"

"Ah shit! Well listen, we're at the movies, could you, just, meet us here?! It's right, down the street, from my place, I promise!"

Although the theater is just down the road from Daven's apartment, he gave the worst directions a person could give and I passed it twice before pulling into the lot. In his defense though, I probably would have passed it anyways because the theater looked like a small tent, placed directly next to a Texas-sized Ace Hardware. The lights were also dimmed on the sign, and unless you lived there, no one would've found it easily. Once I parked, I saw a man standing outside, who could have only been Daven. He was a late-20s man, who was taller than I am, maybe six-feet, clean shaven, and lanky. He waved me down and for the final time, his voice would change. He now spoke exactly like Dale Gribble from King of the Hill, only in an excited and still jumpy manner.

"Alright man! Let's go! I've got popcorn! Beer! And tickets! You missed the beginning but you'll be fine! Don't worry, about paying, either!"

We ran to our film, which was one of only four being shown in the small theater Once seated, our seating arrangement never would change. In the middle of the room, sat the couple from Connecticut, with Connor on the far right, then Megan, myself, and Daven on the far left. To this day, I do not know what that movie is about. We were not the only people in the room, though there weren't too many. I met Daven at the door with a beer in his hand, served in a plastic cup; I learned quickly that he had also gotten Megan to bring him several canned PBRs and half of a handle of Tequila in her purse.

He was about three beers and a few good swigs deep before I realized that he yells like he's being fucked really hard any time anything he finds exciting happens, and at the top of his lungs, it sounded like this: "OH FUCK! AW SHIT! DID YOU FUCKIN' SEE THAT! AW SHIT! SHIT! DAMN! FUCK!!!!" It got so loud, that I was certain you could hear him at the front desk.

It was around this time that Connor got up to go to the bathroom, or so I thought. Then Daven got up to go to the bathroom, or so I thought. And after they'd left, Megan and I looked at each other, both fairly disinterested in the film, and shrugged. She then got up, and did, in fact, use the restroom. Sitting alone, realizing I'd only just met these people, I began to think, "Are they stealing my car?" So I also got up.

They weren't stealing my car, but on my way back to my seat I passed Connor who was very disgruntled, with his arms crossed, and he muddled, "Yeah, it's me from the theater." This was also the first time I had seen the man not in darkness, and learned that he was about my age, maybe five-foot-eight, and had an average build and hair length. He also had a beard.

When I walked back to the film, my seat was still vacant, but Daven and Megan had beaten me back. They had only known each other for six hours or so at this point, but even to total strangers, Connor and Megan were clearly dating one another. With that in mind, I found it very strange to see Daven holding Megan's very uncomfortable hand. I decided to sit down, not only to help her out, but also to simply take my seat. Angry now, Daven reached over me to try again. When he failed, he made eye contact with her, and rapidly moved his hands, in what I believe he thought was sign language. He moved his lips in silence to say, "I am so in love with you" to Megan. When she brushed that off, he muttered to himself and sat back into his chair.

Whenever something Daven found funny in the film happened, he would laugh, and laugh exactly like the cartoon character he replicated. After his confession to Megan, he did just that and slowly rubbed my thigh,

"Dude! What're you doing?"

"Ah shit! Sorry, sorry."

Then he did it again, "Stop!"

"Shit, sorry, sorry, sorry."

I'm not sure if it happened a third time or not, but he looked at me, and loudly exclaimed, "Ah shit! Ah shit! You're not Megan! Ah shit!"

"No, I'm not, can we just watch the damn film and be quiet?"

Somewhere around this time Connor came back, but I had other things to worry about.

Daven tried to play footsies with me, but I kicked out from under him, and told him to watch the movie and be quiet. I didn't just leave at this point because, although unspoken, Megan, Connor, and I were a team now. I wasn't going to leave them alone with a lunatic.

The final action scene of the film happened, and Daven, once again, yelled like he was bed stricken, "AH SHIT! FUCK! LOOK AT THAT FUCKER! AH SHIT SHIT SHIT! FUCK!!!!!"

The credits rolled, the lights came back on, and Connor, Megan, and I stood up to find Daven snoring in his chair. I tapped him and said, "Hey man, it's time to go."

Groggy, he replied, "Ah shit, did, did I fall asleep? Ah shit! Okay."

We walked to the parking lot, and I learned that Connor and Megan had parked on the opposite side of the lot from me. They walked to their car and Daven and I walked toward mine. I had assumed he parked near me, but when he went to open my passenger door, I realized I was wrong. I told him I'd drive him, but there was stuff on the seat and he would have to wait a few minutes for me to move it. He freaked out at this, and Connor drove him. We decided that, although his apartment was close to the theater, it would be a good plan for me to follow them back. I knew then as much as I know now, that the only logical way back was to turn right out of the lot, and of course, we turned left. I followed them into two consecutively closed gas stations. It was a Sunday, now around midnight, in Little Rock, Arkansas; everything was closed. I'm still amazed we got into a theater. At the second lot, I pulled up next to their car, and Daven jumped out of the back seat, leaned into my window, and said very quickly,

"Hey man, hey, I just really, need a cigarette, I can't find any!" I was already smoking a butt, and offered him one, which shocked him, because somehow he didn't understand that I was currently smoking. "If I give you a cigarette, can we please just go back to your apartment?"

When we pulled in front of his complex, Daven was holding his unlit cigarette like a trophy. When he finally lit it, I swear to God, he did it without taking a drag at all, sat it on his steps, and we all walked inside.

One of us said something to the effect of, "Hey man, that's going to burn out if you just leave it there." He went out to smoke finally, closed the door, and I turned to the couple and said, "So is it just me, or is he really fucking weird?"

"Well, he can probably hear you, the door's pretty thin, so let's go upstairs to the guest room where we're staying and talk." Megan is a bit shorter than I am and dressed very hippie like; she was wearing a light shirt with an intentional hole in the back, with relaxed jeans and sneakers. And Connor is a well-groomed, bearded man a little taller than me. The arrangement we agreed upon, was that they would sleep in the guest room while I slept on the couch in the living room. This was only fair because there were two of them and they booked the stay before I had. In a normal arrangement, this would be fine, but in this special case, it wasn't the best of ideas. We talked about how strange he was at the theater, and I learned that as we left, Daven went out of his way to tuck the tag of Megan's bra back into her shirt. Also, that when I saw Connor in the hallway, he was upset because of an argument he and Megan had that had been totally rectified by Daven's intolerable behavior. To my knowledge, the argument never came back up. Daven also spent the entire car ride thanking Connor for the Newport, which is strange seeing as Connor doesn't cigarettes, and it wasn't a Newport. As petty as it sounds, we all decided we could not just leave the man's house because he would likely have written us poor reviews on Couchsurfing, and that review could crippled our immediate future with traveling when we were all very far from our homes.

Daven eventually came back and sensed an awkwardness in the room. To fix that, he tried to get me to go swimming with him, even offering me his swim trunks, and I, as politely as possible, said, "Not tonight man, not even if you paid me."

He gave up and went swimming and immediately texted Megan, "Sorry Max won't leave you guys alone!" He thought I was an awkward third wheel, not that he was a creepy and bothersome man. We agreed that I would sleep in the room with them for the night, on a separate cot. We shared stories of travel, I told them all about my trip so far and Connor took to asking a lot about Alec from Milledgeville and his corsets. They explained that they went to visit Midwestern family of Megan's, and decided to road trip back home.

Eventually Daven came back inside and nearly begged me for another cigarette, I gave it to him mostly because I found these particular cigarettes very disposable. While in Memphis, I picked up a very cheap pack of menthols from the brand Hi-Val. When I lit the first one and took a drag, I pulled it away from my face, looked at it, and out loud said, "That shouldn't taste like this." Hi-Vals taste like generic raw meat, and are very gross. Even to someone as awful as Daven, I would happily bum them one. When he came for a third, however, I declined, lying to the man, and saying I was out of cigarettes. He quickly decided to leave the apartment in conquest of more. It was just after one in the morning after a Sunday night.

Everything was closed, Daven does not drive, and it warms my heart to know that he was drunkenly wandering in this search. I do not know if he was successful, but it doesn't really matter.

In the time he was gone, Connor and Megan told me that before the movie, Daven was a regular guy. There was nothing suspicious about him at all. They then told me two things that would have been red flags to me. The first, was that out of context, Daven very calmly said,

"Guys, you know, I just love drugs. Like all

of them, all the time." And at another point, also out of context, he said,

"You know, I love having sex, with everybody, all the time, always. I just love having a lot of sex." To this day, I don't know how they didn't find those to be flags, but that's their business. Megan had also informed me of where he went when she and Connor also left the theater. The way the room was set up, was there were about eight rows of about fifteen seats, but in between the last row and the projector, there was a small hallway. Daven, with beer in hand, sat cross-legged in that hallway. Surely he could not see the screen, but he was there, alone, for at least ten minutes before returning to his seat. The man never left the room. We believe that he was probably on ecstasy. Together, we decided that we would lock the door, and plan to wake up and leave before he got up, saying we had plans to get to.

When we woke up, Connor and Megan decided that instead of leaving immediately and avoiding potential danger, they had to individually shower. Again, I wasn't going to leave them alone, but I urged them against this. They didn't know it, but I had gone a couple days and a lot of sweat driving without a shower, but they did in fact clean themselves.

Of course, Daven had woken up by this point. We trudged our belongings downstairs, awkwardly hugged the man, and closed the door behind us. Megan, Connor, and I had become pretty close by this point, and I hugged her and shook his hand. We got in our respective cars, and as the perfect icing on the cake, mine had died overnight. I flagged them down, realizing that I would rather be in the desert than have to ask for Daven's help. Luckily, Connor MacGyvered the car to life and we ended up getting breakfast together. I still talk to them to this day.

After leaving them, I did see Little Rock High, which still operates, as well as the museum across the street. I was blown away by all of what Little Rock is, between history and creepery. Frightening encounters aside, I highly recommend the city's historical side to anyone who has interest in Civil Rights.

Mid-day Parade

After leaving the horrible Daven behind in
Little Rock, I was headed for New Orleans. I
was excited to see the Cajun land, but didn't
quite know what I'd be in store for. I'd been
unable to find anyone on Couchsurfing to agree
to house me, so back to living in my car is what
I had in store. I found myself in a parking lot on
Canal street, which runs through the center of
downtown NOLA. The lot was just outside of
the major downtown area and allowed patrons to
park for twelve hours for three dollars. I would
find myself sleeping in this lot for several nights
to come. Canal street takes you to the French
Quarter, Bourbon street, and nearly anything
else you could want to see in town.

As soon as I left my car I was faced with the
smell, the smell of New Orleans. It is a putrid
piss, shit, and vomit smell; night and day, inside
and out, the smell does not leave. Within a few
minutes of walking around I knew I was in the
dirtiest place I had ever seen. I know that

Katrina damaged the city immensely and our government did not clean the way they ought to have.

Poor circumstance in mind, New Orleans is a very gross place to be. The smell is unbearable, everything feels dirty, the streets are too loud, and I swear it left a dirty taste in my mouth. I have never been in a place that so vibrantly smelled like piss, shit, and vomit at the same time, indoors and out. If I were a filmmaker, I would love NOLA, as it is pretty to the eyes, beautiful even. When you're at the dock, the water looks gorgeous and so do the ships. Once night falls, the streets around Bourbon are fantastic to look at as the drunken people wander, the prostitutes advertise, and the strippers and pimps offer specials to lonely looking passersby. Even the obvious tourist confusion would capture well on film. Unfortunately, I'm not a film maker and the negative scent outweighed the sight for me.

One of the truly prettiest things in New Orleans were their impromptu mid-day parades. I found myself walking in front of a hotel on

Canal street. Two men on high stilts dressed in bright green and purple outfits that look like muumuus came outside and started talking to each other. I suppose you could've called them *stilt men.* Before I knew it, an entire marching band had pooled outside, and they were followed by what must have been nearly every guest of the hotel. When a third characterized man came outside, they lined up in the middle of traffic, and marched away. No one else looked twice at this, but I had never seen such a thing. These parades are known to happen all the time, and they mesmerized me.

There are also men who paint their clothes and bodies in gold or silver paint and stand as though they're statues. A few of them tricked me until they winked at me. One of the men, painted in silver, put himself on the edge of traffic with a fake dog on a leash. If he moved closer to the street the dog would have been annihilated. I'm still confused about why he was posing there to begin with.

I slept in my car every night in NOLA. I would trek myself back to the parking lot, make up my back seat, and get stoned. The lot was huge; I'm sure it can fit 500 cars easily, and I parked in the direct middle of the lot, away from anything and under several lights. For protections sake, I even became friendly with the tow truck guy. I would get high so I could sleep and I kept my knife under my pillow. Fortunately, I never needed it. Unfortunately, every morning the sweltering sun woke me up. Although I cracked a window, after the sun had been up for no more than ten minutes, my car was a hot box, and I was drenched in sweat.

Sleeping in my car, my food consisted mostly of the canned foods and the snacks I had gathered along the way. When I didn't want those, I ate at McDonalds and I-Hop on Canal street, which was convenient because those were also my changing rooms. I found myself fitting right in with the local homeless people; I smelled, I seemed lost, and I was often stoned. The town has homeless people like most towns have coffee shops; they're everywhere. It's sad, but, I found myself happy to see that these people were usually positive and seemed happy to be alive. I come from a town with many homeless people, from a crazy man idolized only after his murder, to a man called Hands, because he talks in mumbles and waves his hands over his head year round, and has a leathery tan. I feel horribly for homeless people. In NOLA, they are much more engaging and part of the culture. I had a run-in with a large black homeless man who named himself Dan Dan the Shoe Man.

Dan Dan stopped me on the street and said to me, "I bet I can tell ya where ya gotcha shoes. If I do, you let me clean them for a fee."

"I'm not sure where I bought them, man."

"Nah, where you got 'em. Not bought 'em."

"Okay where?"

"You gots 'em on your feet!" He went on to laugh, squirt shampoo on my shoes and scrub them. "It'll be forty dollars now."

"I'm not giving you forty dollars for that man!"

"I see that fifty in your wallet there. Give it here!"

"My wallet is in my pocket! I'm not giving you forty dollars for this!"

"You gots to. I told you where ya gots ya shoes, didn't I?"

"You made me laugh, so I'll give you ten, okay?" I opened my wallet to hand him ten dollars.

"Nah man, I see you gots that twenty I'm needin'. Let's have it here."

"Take the ten man, that's all you're getting out of me," I handed him the bill and walked away, smiling at his joke, and upset that I got hustled. I went on to have the best gumbo I've ever eaten at a small restaurant near Bourbon street. I ordered a small bowl of the soup and loved each bite of it. The servers of the place kept waiting for me to order more food or a drink. I guess gumbo is usually only an appetizer there. I paid and left them a tip for the food, and they begrudgingly asked me to "please come back soon!"

****

On my final night there, I decided to sleep in a cheap motel outside of town. It was one of those motels where men take hookers for the night, a little bit better than the ones with ten-minute-rates, but not by much. Everything had to be paid in cash and my room didn't have a telephone; someone had stolen it. When I brought this up to the clerk, she said, "If you really need it, you can share with a neighbor tenant for the night."

"I'm all set with that, but is my room a smoking room? I'd really like an ashtray."

"Honey, all the rooms are non-smoking and all the rooms are smoking. I'll have a cleaning lady move the sign and I'll fetch you a tray."

I found myself very fortunate to be a smoker here, the poor non-smokers had no idea what they were faced with. I found myself smoking and writing for most of the night. Exhausted of the sweaty awakenings I'd been having, I also made a mess of the bathroom and shaved my head with the clippers I'd brought from home for this exact reason.

When I woke up the next morning, nearly bald, I headed back to NOLA for a final time. I had been trying to play open mics the whole time I'd been in town but they were always for people over twenty-one, or were booked full by the time I showed up. I decided that on this last day, I'd play one successfully. I found a small club having a comedian exclusive open mic that night. I put my name on the list and it seemed like an amateur night, exactly what I was looking for. After the first comedian went up, I realized that the majority of the other talent weren't going to be a problem, but what was a bittersweet problem was that an upcoming comedian was there. She was only in town to film with Key and Peele, and was soon to be leaving NOLA for a tour in Canada with Louis C.K. and Gilbert Gottfried, or some people like that. Her name was Tiffany Haddish. She stopped by because it was something to do and tried out an hours' worth of new material on all of us. She was hilarious and I'm thrilled to have met her, but it made it difficult for newcomers to get on that stage. By the time I finished my set, it was about two in the morning.

Because NOLA doesn't close like Boston or Philadelphia, everyone was still out in the streets. I got in my car and drove to a nearby gas station where I met a homeless fellow looking to clean cars for whatever he could get. After he begged me to clean the car, I told him I'd clean it, but I liked his attitude and gave him about half a pack of cigarettes and a lighter. He couldn't have been happier, and thanked me more than most people thank anyone. My car filled, I began to drive through the night, north, to McKinney Texas to meet the Rodger family.

Mr. Rodgers in Tokyo

I knew I had to turn the tape way down as I entered the neighborhood of the Rodger's family in McKinney Texas. McKinney is just outside of Dallas, and isn't exactly a poor community, but upon turning onto the street adjacent to theirs, I realized that these people are stupid rich. The roads rapidly went from being owned by well off people to being owned by people whose great grandchildren would never have a financial worry. Listening to a 1993 rap cassette in a '96 beater car, I felt misplaced. The house I'd be staying in was nothing short of a mansion; it was enormous, with an all stone exterior, ten-foot-tall front door, balconies galore, and a yard to match. This was just what you could tell from the curb; and in a poorer town it would've been used to house eight or ten apartments for mid-sized families. I waited almost no time at all for Karen to answer.

My father had always said, about my trip, that he would help me with places to stay as much as he could. Karen, the mother of the family, had graduated high school with my father in Wyomissing, PA. This seemed normal, that a long-lost high-school friend, re-connected through social media, would be up for hosting their lost friend's now adult son on a long trip. I had that in the back of my head until my arrival, when I very quickly learned, that this was simply not the case.

Karen welcomed me into the home with open arms, I said hello to her dogs and then she asked me to help her make the bed of the room I was to stay in. At this point we began talking about each other, as we had only met through brief texts before this. I told her about my comedy and that I'm a drummer. She told me that she teaches yoga for a living, that only one of her two daughters and her husband were home during my stay, and her mother was also visiting from Florida. She would go on to ask about my father, basic questions, like what he does for work, where he lives, how many siblings I have, and anything about his relationship with my mother. By the second or third question, I knew exactly what Karen was going to say next, which was along the lines of,

"Your dad and I never really knew each other in high school, yeah we went there together, but I didn't go to that school until my junior year, and we never really talked more than maybe a couple times. I always assumed you lived in Reading, not Boston!" Karen and my father, now over 30 years out of high school, were total strangers.

Once I met the rest of the family I learned a lot about them very quickly. Mr. Rodgers was Mister Business Man, and didn't really have much else to talk about. He told me he was a CEO of a major company that I'm not allowed to tell other people about, so let's just say, in an agreeable comparison, that it was CVS. Not only was he CEO, he was the third chair in the company worldwide. He has money for lifetimes. The daughter that I met was about my age and was going to college. When I asked her what she was studying and why, she told me she went because she was bored. She had no idea of the struggle most Americans go through to get an education.

I found the grandmother to be the most interesting of the bunch. She was a Chilean immigrant, who came to this country before Karen had been born. She informed me that a Brit had taught her English upon her arrival, but for some reason, she had a very thick German-American accent. I asked her about this, and she didn't understand what I was trying to say. Not only had no one ever told her this before, but she hardly knows any Germans.

On my first night, we went out to dinner at a local burger restaurant. When I saw that my burger, fries, and Pepsi cost just over twenty-five dollars, I was shocked. It was a good burger, but not one worth so much money; it was comparable to a Fuddruckers meal. After Mr. Rodgers insisted on paying the one hundred and fifty dollar bill, which I could not have even dented, the daughter took it upon herself to demand he help her find a specific kind of lipstick that was soon to be discontinued. The two of them went off looking for that, the grandmother went clothes shopping and Karen and I got a cup of eight-dollar coffee. We talked a lot about life, relationship problems and travel for me, and on her end, we talked thoroughly about her other daughter's living situation in Boulder, Colorado. The issue wasn't necessarily about where she was living, but that her lease was up, and her landlord didn't like that she had a cat. She was being kicked out. I suppose that wasn't really the problem either, the real issue was finding her a house by the end of the week. That's right, Karen and her husband's solution to the eviction was to buy a house. The money was there, it was just about finding the right house for her quickly!

****

The following day, I found myself swimming in the pool with Mr. Rodgers. He came to me in confidence and told me that he was going to leave CVS soon because a bigger company gave him a better offer, but I couldn't tell anyone about the switch. He also started to complain to me that he had to fly to Tokyo in a couple days for a conference for CVS, saying,

"I've gone so many times, I like Tokyo, but I'm sick of going."

Once inside again, I found myself in the kitchen with Karen, her daughter, and mother. We were talking about a boy that the daughter had gone to high school with that had passed away. It was very sad and she and Karen began to choke up. Although this family was stupid rich, this conversation was the ultimate example of why I would watch them if they were a sitcom. Grandma, in her late sixties/early seventies, says very inappropriate things. She's far from dementia stricken; she just doesn't know how to talk about things she knows little about. So, while everyone was sad and on the verge of tears, Grandma leaned in real close to all of us, and in her German accent, said to us almost like she was asking a question,

"You know, I've always wanted to make scones."

None of us knew what to do with that information and stopped talking, smiled a bit, and went on with our business. I, personally, left the group so I could write that down.

That night, Mr. Rodgers told me I had to leave in two mornings because he was going to Tokyo

and Karen was going to Nashville. She was
going there to buy a new castle to live in for
when he made the switch between companies.
Adding, that if he got there and didn't like it,
they would simply sell that house too and find a
better one close by. When I finally did leave
them, I left Karen a thank you note, started the
car, and more specifically my cassette, which
had Snoop kick back in where it left off.

Adobe the Beautiful

After leaving the Rodger's family I drove to New Mexico, where I would be staying with a Couchsurfer named Connor. The plan we agreed upon was that I'd stay three days and two nights. Connor lived in Santa Fe, although he has since moved. The north border of Texas and New Mexico is also the dividing line between the central and mountain time zones. As I hope many readers will eventually see for themselves, that border is also the difference between dreary hot deserts and beautiful, green, cavernous valley ways. I swear to God, it's even sunnier in New Mexico. Sure, you're still in the desert, but it's different somehow. Almost like that hour difference gives the land of New Mexico more life and happiness. While driving on I-40, for what seems like an eternity, it all changes magically as soon as you cross into the western state.

Like most of the states south of the Mason-Dixon line, New Mexico does not really believe in street lights. By this point, I was mostly used to that, but on this night it was especially bad. On the tail end of my driving, around eight that night, driving north on US-84, it began to rain lightly. Realizing I was the only car on the highway that night and that my directions were nothing short of mediocre, I was not a huge fan of my surroundings. By the time I had turned off the highway and onto the long road to Connor's home, it had begun to lightning and downpour. Even Connor would later admit that this was unusual for that time of year.

When I found his home, I called him and was told to park on the street, as he would be out shortly. Not only was Santa Fe much greener, and friendlier to the eyes than McKinney, it was also much cooler on this rainy night. The temperature could not have passed 60 degrees. I didn't think much of that but found myself cold for the first time in months. Looking around, I was also very happy to see Connor's apartment; I had never seen an adobe building before.

When he came out to meet me, he looked much like I'd imagined; Connor is a Caucasian man a little taller than me, who has brown hair and wears flip flops. He is also a little idiosyncratically flamboyant. I apologized for my late arrival and he, as a kind host, told me not to worry about it. He lived in a three-family apartment, but like none I have ever seen before or since.

When someone says "three family apartment," they typically think of a three floor building, each floor rented out to tenants. Connor happened to live alone. In a three-story building, his apartment would be an attic. Maybe this building would also have a basement for collective storage, or a washroom somewhere too. None of that describes Connor's building. The wall facing the street and where you would at first glance think the front door is, is the first apartment. Beside that wall, moving back, away from the road, is what one would again, at a glance, think is a driveway. Instead, it is a very crowded parking lot for all tenants. In the middle of this parking lot, where the building narrows slightly, is the entrance to the second apartment, and behind that in the lot, in the very back of the building, was Connor's even smaller apartment. I say the building narrows, but in reality it looks like someone molded three buildings and glued them together, or like three lazy Chinese Nesting Dolls laying down.

Inside the apartment, Connor kindly showed me around; when you open the front door, you're in the living room and kitchen. For some reason, which Connor has never understood, the laundry machines were stacked on top of one another in the back on the living room half of the one single room. He explained that I could help myself to water from the sink and showed me the cupboards where cups and general things were. He pointed to the futon in the living room and told me I'd be sleeping there.

"I'm sorry I don't have something better. It's only me here, and in this place, I don't usually let more than one guest visit at once. Except for one time when three guys from Iceland all crashed on that futon because they were in desperate need of a roof."

This seemed silly to me; the futon is not large by any means, and when I think of Icelanders, I think of large men.

I laughed, "Hey man, thanks for letting me stay here at all, anything helps!"

He pointed out that he was growing various plants in the living room, which had a television and some books as well. He pointed past the room into his bedroom and told me the bathroom was through there. That's the whole apartment. I suppose it's a studio apartment that just didn't have quite enough room. I noticed also that there were no corners here, just rounded clay and to this day, I'm not sure how the electrical outlets work, assuming they were put in after the building had been there a while. It really was solid clay.

****

The next morning, Connor explained that while he was working, he didn't want me in his home. I, understandably, took that chance to explore the city and such. He suggested a coffee shop, Whoo's Donuts and the Turquoise Trail to me. We also agreed to see a film after he finished work.

As I drove around Santa Fe, I started to realize that the whole city was covered in adobe buildings. I was, and still am, mesmerized by this notion. Nowhere else in this world have I seen so many buildings look so old fashioned. Whoo's Donuts was across the street from a beautiful park where children played and elderly women walked their dogs. Inside the shop, I found myself looking fondly at the owner's friend's art, of which there was plenty. All of the paintings, sculptures, and sketches were of dying people or skeletons in strangely happy situations. They all had very vibrant colors and somehow belonged in this very hippy coffee place. They had a bookshelf that instructed visitors to, "read at your own pleasure. Take a book- leave a book" I didn't have a book to contribute at the time, so I ended up drinking my raspberry flavored coffee and reading the midsection of "Slaughterhouse Five," a book that I've read all of but only through scenarios like this.

The Turquoise Trail is something I recommend to most people. It connects Santa Fe with Albuquerque on mostly dirt roads that used to be riddled with the valuable stone. Some people believe there is still turquoise there. Many cavernous craters and older village homes line the trail, but, unfortunately, it ends near downtown Albuquerque. In the early 20th century, Albuquerque was a hub for railroad systems and industry. Now, it is left as a rundown version of its former self.

****

When I did meet back up with Connor, I explained how cool it was that all of Santa Fe was made of adobe.

"Yeah, I thought that too when I moved here, and then I did some investigating. It turns out, sometime in the last twenty years or so, the city decided to capitalize on tourism. They passed a law that forces all buildings to be made of adobe. They adobed historical buildings made of other materials! The Walmart, grocery store, and theater are all adobe here! It's cool, but kinda crazy."

I find this silly; an entire city forces all of their buildings to be made of one material capitalize on it, and it works. It's a genius plan that wouldn't work many places. As we went to the theater, I realized further that Connor was right; I tried and couldn't find a single building not covered in clay. Once inside, we decided to see *Jurassic World*, the newest film in the set. After, we got some beers, and laughed about how much the film screams like an 80s movie. The product placement, especially for Coca-Cola, structured gender roles, and overall plot, make it seem like a film written thirty years ago, but with modern CGI effects. As weirdly old-fashioned of a film as it was, we both thoroughly enjoyed it. The next morning, I headed north for Denver.

Cookie

While staying with Connor, I started talking with Jeremy, the final Couchsurfing host of my trip. Jeremy lives in Erie, Colorado, and replied quickly to my request to visit him.

"Hey. I might have a favor to ask in exchange for a place to stay. Please call me when you have a chance."

I started to wonder what on earth he could be asking me to do that he couldn't explain in a text. Having already stayed with many Couchsurfers that weren't exactly trustworthy, I began to worry about what craziness this guy could be up to. However, when it came right down to it, all I was asked to do was call him and if he wanted me to smuggle drugs or something awful, I would just say I made other arrangements.

When I called the man, he asked me if I could drive him and his children to the airport on that Friday, at five in the morning so they could leave for their family vacation. The plan was for me to arrive Wednesday night.

"Sure man, I don't have a ton of room, but we can squeeze together in my car and then I'll just be on my way."

"No, no! You can use my truck to drive us if you feel comfortable and then you can stay here for a few more days if you'd like."

"We haven't even met yet! Are you sure you'll be okay with a stranger in your home without you for a few days?"

"If I feel good about you, then sure! It'll be fine. We'll see when you get here, but I get a good vibe from you. I have to drop my kids off at their mother's before you get here tonight, so call me to make sure I'm home when you arrive. I hope that's not a problem."

"Thank you so much! That sounds fine to me, I'll see you tonight."

****

I arrived in the small town early and got myself some dinner at a McDonald's. After leaving the restaurant, a homeless woman asked me for a cigarette. On my trip I held a general rule, which I still hold today, if a homeless person seems like a good and interesting person,

I'll give them some money or a cigarette if they ask. This woman was down on her luck and just needed a pick-me-up; if I didn't have to be somewhere at the time, I would have stuck around and hung out for a few minutes. Although in a terrible situation, she was charming and someone I would have liked to know. She didn't need any food, just a butt. So I gave the woman my last Pall Mall, which I quickly found myself replacing with Camel Blue's, because they were the cheapest in the state.

When I showed up to Jeremy's cul-de-sac, I parked in front of his two-story home. He and his dog, greeted me at the door and welcomed me to their kitchen table. We talked about his children, and him splitting them with his ex. Jeremy felt very comfortable with me staying there alone, and asked me to have dinner with him and his kids on Thursday night. He didn't want me smoking indoors, but didn't care what else I did. His kids loved meeting Couchsurfers.

"Let me show you where you'll be staying," He directed me toward the basement, "It's finished down here, most of my guests stay in this room."

The basement had its own bathroom, common room, and a bedroom, as well as, "And those are my instruments. Do you play anything?" He waved his hand in the direction of a drum kit, guitar, and bass.

"Yeah, I'm also a drummer actually."

"Feel free to use whatever you'd like while you're here! I want you to feel at home."

This gesture was like telling a bodybuilder they could use weights for the first time in years. I couldn't wait to use his kit. I'd brought a snare drum with me, but it's nothing like playing on a full set.

"Are you an outdoorsy guy? I recommend the Rockies a lot as well as a park in Boulder!"

When I was there, he told me what the trail's name was. It's Native American and because I only heard it spoken, not written, I've never been sure what it is.

"All I ask of you is that you replace what you take. If you eat food, buy something similar to leave behind. Contribute when you can. I basically live on oatmeal and coffee; I hope you like coffee."

"Yeah that all sounds great! Thank you for being so generous! And yes, I'll likely compete with you on how much coffee we can both drink."

"Cool! Oh, I almost forgot, did you come here for the pot? I don't really like it, but when people visit me they get excited about it. It is great weed out here, but getting high just isn't my thing."

"No, I'm only twenty so I can't even buy it. I'm mostly here for the Rockies and to explore Denver, I hope that's close to here. I mean, I do smoke weed, but I didn't come for it."

"Well, Denver and Boulder are both about a half hour from here, just in opposite directions. I can buy you some weed if you'd like. Just let me know what you want and pay me back. I pass a place every day on the construction job I'm working on. I can get it for you tomorrow."

"Wow, sure! That'd be fantastic man!"

"Cool, well I'm gonna head to bed, I have work at four in the morning. Make yourself at home!"

****

I spent the next day walking around Denver. I checked out some book stores, saw the Robin Williams' Mork mural, and found myself there on the day of a Gay-pride parade. I arrived after the march, but the banners and flags were still everywhere I looked. It was neat; I had been unaware of the parade, but it seemed to be an almost regular event in town. Even more impressive, was the fact that aside from the festivities, Denver is the only place I've ever been where everyone is accepted. Being attracted to men, a lot of the time, I almost have to hide finding a guy cute. It is the only place I've ever been or heard of where you don't even have a good guess at anyone's sexual preferences or identities. Normally, you know, or at least have an idea, of who might have interest in you by looking at them. Here, anyone could have interest in you, or not. Racially, as well, I never saw anyone look down or act poorly toward someone of a different racial background. In my hometown, I know several people to use the phrase *I see in black and white, not color* all the time. By this, they usually mean that it isn't a person's appearance that they judge, but their actions. In Denver, I believed this could be their city motto. That ambiguity shows a town's acceptance of whatever you could throw at it, and we need more places like this.

The time came for dinner with Jeremy's family and I headed back to the house. Once again, he greeted me at the door with Cookie, the dog, and introduced me to his children. He has two daughters, six and thirteen, and his middle child is a boy named Kyle. He's nine and my favorite because he reminds me of a nine year old me. After we ate a beautifully grilled steak dinner, the children started yelling that they wanted ice cream. Jeremy was stressed about packing for their flight the next morning, so I volunteered to drive to the store for the treat. Noting that I could only fit one of the children in the car with me, Kyle was the one to go.

"Alright Kyle, you need to direct me to the store, I'm not totally sure where we're going."

"It's just down here," We could see about six bicyclers riding down the road, "Max, if you hit these people, a portal will open up and we will be there quicker. I promise."

This was something, as a nine-year-old, I definitely said to an adult in the car. I would have been joking, of course, but it still would have been a statement I would have tossed out there.

I decided to antagonize Kyle, "Alright, but if I hit them and the police come, I'm going to tell them that you said to hit them."

When I was nine, the thought of jail freaked me out, I would have panicked. This is where I learned that Kyle is like a smarter nine-year-old me,

"Okay, Max, but when the cops come and you tell them that, I'm going to tell them that I'm nine and you hit those people!"

I laughed at the kid, and we got the ice cream, injury free, from the Walgreens in town. This Walgreens was about the only business I ever saw in Erie. Kyle picked out an orange cream flavor and we returned to present this to his sisters and father. The girls enjoyed it, and Jeremy ran around trying to pack. I took to occupying the children, and introducing them to the wonders of Trivial Pursuit; I brought the children's version from my car, and we played until their bedtimes, which were shortly followed by mine and their father's.

When I woke the next morning, it was before the kids were awake. In that brief moment of groggy and calmness, I had a cup of coffee with Jeremy, who handed me a bag he had bought for me. Inside were a canister of marijuana gummy bears and some weed for smoking. I paid him back and hid the stuff from his children in my luggage. Then he woke the kids up, we loaded everything into his truck, and in a daze, all drove down the highway as the sun rose. Jeremy drove there, and after dropping them at the terminal, I sat in the front seat for the first time. What I didn't realize until now was that the truck was very old and filled, in the bed, roof, and sides with construction equipment. I'd only driven a truck a couple times, but the fact that I could only see out of the windshield and part of the driver's side mirror, made the experience all the worse. I drove slowly down the highway, now crowded with early morning commuters, and eventually made it safely back to his home, parked, and promptly went back to sleep.

When I woke up and walked up stairs, I was greeted by a boy about Kyle's age, feeding Cookie. He looked at me, "Who are you?"

"I'm Jeremy's friend, I'm crashing here for a few days."

"Well why aren't you feeding the dog?"

"They wanted Cookie to have the same person taking care of her, and I'd be leaving before they return."

"Oh okay, well, bye," He hurried out of the house and I made more coffee before heading into the Rocky Mountains. I found myself wandering around the bottom of the mountains, in the forest, for hours and hours. It was a hot and sunny summer day, and I was so thrilled to be in such a beautiful place. By the time I had decided to climb back up to the top, the sun was starting to set. The most surreal situation of my life was standing, looking at wild cows, and wearing shorts, while holding snow on top of these mountains. I have never felt so absorbed by nature as I did right then.

When I got back to Jeremy's house, I had forgotten how to open the garage. I had no key to the home and was effectively locked out. After trying all other options, I crawled in through Cookie's doggy door and was surprised that the neighbors didn't call the police. Inside, I figured out the garage's trick so I wouldn't face the same problem again. Cookie had clearly not been fed a second time that day since I'd left; I believe the boy never returned.

I ate some of the edibles Jeremy bought me and got higher than I have ever been. They tasted exactly like Sour Patch Kids. He recommended I eat half of one, and instead, I ate two. All I really remember is watching reruns of sitcoms

on my laptop and writing some more.
Eventually, the weed put me to sleep. When I
woke up, a man was upstairs feeding Cookie,

"Who are you?" He asked me in a very
concerned and demanding tone.

"I'm Max. I'm Jeremy's friend and I'll be
crashing here for a few days."

"Why aren't you feeding the dog?"

"He said he wanted a consistent dog watcher
for Cookie. I'm leaving before he returns, but
I'm not sure that matters anymore."

"Okay, have a good day," He left and shut
the door behind him.

That morning, I started talking with my
friends from home, Tyler and Shane, who
wanted to meet me in San Francisco for a
vacation for themselves and to hang out for the
first time in months. We started planning, and
that night they both had booked Red Eye flights
for just after I was to be in Phoenix. I was very
excited to hear about the trip, and after making
more coffee, I ended our conversation so I could
go to a park Jeremy had recommended in
Boulder.

When I arrived there, I realized that Jeremy had tricked me a little; it wasn't a park like a field, but another hiking trail, specifically, the Chautauqua trail. This trail is almost entirely uphill and about two miles long. It truly is beautiful, except for at the bottom of the trail. At the beginning of the trail, not hidden at all, a woman was blowing a man, and when I saw them, they promptly looked at me like I was in the wrong. Just past them, in the middle of the trail, was a scene I can't make much sense of, but a man was standing in front of a woman with her vagina hanging out, almost blowing in the wind. Although almost majestic, I'm not sure what they were doing, but again, they looked at me like I was in the wrong.

Once past them, the trail was less sex orientated, and much more nature oriented, which kind of sounds like the same thing. The trail is difficult at parts, but once at the top, you can see clear into Denver, and the air is fresher than normal. It was there, that I decided adult Denver and Boulder residents have no excuse to not be in pristine shape; the only two things to do are hike amazing trails and smoke the best weed in the nation.

That night, I played an open mic at a burger shop in Denver. I told all new stories, all from my trip, which included Little Rock, Florida, McKinney, and concluded with my stay so far in Colorado. I told the crowd about my walk that day on the Boulder trail and the people having sexual days out. The crowd laughed, and when I asked an audience member, I learned they laughed because I was an outsider, everyone fucks there, except tourists of course. That night I also heard the best joke at an open mic I've ever heard. It was from a woman comedian, who said,

"I'm sick of men saying they're getting their dick wet, not because it's hurtful to women, but because we don't have an equivalent. Now I'm going to start telling people, 'I need to get my pussy packed.'" I still laugh at this joke as hard as I did that night.

That night I played Jeremy's drum set for hours, got stoned one more time, and packed my things. No one had fed Cookie again, and I felt bad; maybe after I left she wouldn't eat much until they got home. The following morning, for the last time, I was faced with a new dog watcher. This time it was a girl, and again, she said to me, in an alarmed state, "Who are you?!" Exhausted of this conversation, I sighed, and rolled my eyes,

"I'm Max, Jeremy's friend, and I was crashing here. He wanted consistent dog watchers and I'm leaving today, before he returns. Of course, this never really mattered."

"Oh, okay, well have a good trip. Bye."

She left, and so did I.

Alone

While I was in Erie one day, after Jeremy left, I hit the point that every solo long term traveler hits. Absolute aloneness. I would go on and ask other travelers about this, and we all agree, there is no word for the notion I experienced, but it happened to all of us. In my case, I was taking a shower in Jeremy's basement, and it dawned on me that I had not seen a familiar face in over six weeks. Shy of a few days, no one within hundreds of miles really knew anything about me. That feeling crippled me for about a half hour, and I sat down on the edge of his tub until the water went cold.

I was sitting until eventually Cookie, Jeremy's dog, showed up. I petted the animal for a little bit and got comfort in that. I realized that this wasn't a depression. Depression lasts a while and is usually loaded with anxiety, at least in my case. This notion, however, was an absolute aloneness, a feeling where you know you are the only person you know and will see for a long time. It is also one of the strangest feelings I had ever experienced. It was something I wished someone had warned me of, because I didn't know how to handle it. So for any future travelers, watch out. When I left on this trip, I had been looking to find myself, and the best way to do that was to get as far away from any sort of comfort zone as I could and see how I reacted. In this specific instance, I reacted with tears, followed by countless cigarettes and some weed on a stranger's back deck.

In other instances where I felt this alone on the trip, I would react by driving faster or in a more specific direction. Sometimes I would call someone I knew, for comfort. It is a good feeling though; I made it sound murky, but in actuality, it shows any given individual how they must handle themselves, and who they actually are. In my case, I was a cigarette addict who needed travel and eventual companionship. These are things I could and did live contently with. It was not long after this that I began driving again, leaving Colorado behind. Be wary future travelers.

It's a Plain, Dry Death

After leaving Cookie behind, I drove to
Phoenix through Utah, hoping to see the Four
Corners before arriving at my uncle's house. He
and I had been talking a lot on the phone, and
decided that instead of me going alone, we
would drive up to the Grand Canyon together
after I arrived. The communication died out
quickly after entering Utah, though. The state is
high elevated, and filled with canyons; reception
is horrible. The first few canyons I saw were
beautiful and I stopped to take photos. At most
of them vendors sell jewelry and rugs that look
Native American, but usually aren't. Gypsy like
people run these stands; and I took photos of
them too. However, by the fiftieth, hundredth,
and what seemed like the millionth canyon, I
was exhausted of them. Around this time, I also
came to the realization that at most times, I was
the only car on the road. The entire time I spent
there, I saw less than two dozen cars, and maybe
three dozen people. I spent a day and a half in

the state. The only establishments I saw were a McDonald's, an Arby's, two gas stations, and a Motel 6. I used all of them.

Not only was I the only one on the road, it was also one hundred and ten degrees outside, at all times. The heat was dry, which sounds alright to most people, but it was the driest heat I have ever experienced. With no exaggeration, the spit in my mouth evaporated! I was driving with the windows halfway down, to keep some sand out, but to get an air flow; I still had no air conditioning from back in Florida.

Salt Lake City might be the best place on Earth, but I never saw it. I was driving through the southern 300 miles of the state. Once night fell, I was fortunate enough to find the Motel 6, and crash there for the night; day driving was difficult enough, I didn't want to drive in pitch black that night. Utah is yet another state to not use any street lights.

The motel was run by two Indian women, who spoke very little English. After spending some time there, I realized that they and I were the only people in the whole building, and the only ones I ever saw. That being said, it was strange that they insisted on giving me the handicapped room. Dozens of other rooms were vacant that night, but they insisted this was the one for me. The difference, in this motel, between a normal room and this one, was that mine had metal bars randomly placed on the walls everywhere, and extra telephones, in case anything went wrong. It still only had one twin sized bed, which made me wonder what person, so handicapped they need all these necessities, would be staying someplace alone.

The special bathroom was by far my favorite part of the room. The entire room was basically the shower. A curtain did divide the shower from the sink and toilet, but it had no wall blocking the water from getting everywhere. This was intentional, the only drain was in the center of the room, but it wasn't at a decline. The room got soaked whenever the shower ran for only a couple minutes. When used by its marketed tenants, it works well, because it has a detachable shower head. I assume the tenants are usually wheelchair bound, which proves a difficulty, because it's resting at normal height. After I took a weird shower, slept very well in a dusty bed, and paid my bill, I got food at the McDonald's and used the only other gas station I would see until Arizona, about a hundred miles later.

Back on the, very literally, dusty trail, I was driving for what seemed like forever without seeing much of anything. I was very sweaty and decided to call my Uncle and ask to go to the Four Corners together, because I just needed to see civilization sooner than later. If I were to have gone to the corners first, it would have been well into the night by the time I arrived; once in Arizona, I still had about 150 miles left before my uncle's home in Scottsdale. He agreed, and after the call I realized, that if I broke down, no one would ever find me and AAA likely doesn't exist much there anyways. For the only time on the trip, I thought to myself, "If I break down here, I will die in this heat and it will be a plain, dry death."

Technology

While staying in Phoenix, I found myself physically lonely and decided to use Tinder, the dating/hookup app. There, I began talking with a seemingly lovely girl named Rita, who very early on, told me that she was transgender. This was good news, by being pansexual, not only do your genitals not really matter to me, but transgender people all have one thing in common; they all have something interesting to talk about. I met Rita, at a Coffee Bean and Tea Leaf shop, and I learned that she was the foul smell to the house of transgender people. That is to say, she was the part you would simply avoid if you knew better.

Have you ever been on a date where about eight seconds into it, you wished you could politely leave and never return? This was just like that. Early on, Rita started gossiping to me about people I would never meet and celebrities I have only a vague understanding of. She complained about college, and of a major I forgot as soon as she said it. She bickered to herself about several part time jobs that she had and hated. The only thing I remember about her jobs from the date was that she was sometimes a nude model for art students; she's the only model I've met of that sort. She constantly kept throwing in the fact that her penis still functions with its sperm and semen. She looked very feminine. This should have been a red flag, but, I didn't think much of it. Sure that's fine and dandy, but let's move on.

"You know, I'm going to freeze some of my sperm before I become a full woman," she said very proudly.

I suppose, if I were in those shoes, I may do the same, thinking, perhaps I'd end up falling in love with a woman and we would want a child with both our genetics; I'd have some backed up. It was now that she, without blinking an eye, said the single craziest thing anyone has ever said to me.

"Once my procedure is finished, I'm going to go to Germany, where they have the technology." She said *the technology* with pride, and I'm sorry, but no, they do not have the technology. "I'll go there and they can give me an implant womb. I'm going to go over there and have my own kids!"

This woman plans to go through a very difficult form of cloning, more than once, to procreate, if that's the term you'd like to use. My mind began racing, would it even survive, if it were to, what would be its serious complications and what generation later would they just stop functioning at all. I started to wonder further when she went on to say the second craziest thing anyone has ever said to me. From my own personal experience, transgender peoples are much like other minority groups; in a given region, they usually all know each other. They may not all be friendly, but they're aware of each other.

"I have this friend who is also male to female trans," she said to me, "But they're just past the point of a functioning penis. It's still hanging there, but it only pisses, nothing sexual at all about the thing. I can't believe she didn't freeze her sperm too! Why the hell wouldn't she want her own kids?! God I can't fucking believe her!"

It would've been rude to leave right away, so I waited a few minutes, changed the topic a bit, then stood up, shook her hand, and said I had to leave. I have not spoken to her since, and I suspect, the next time I hear her name it will be on a headline, reading, "Crazy Lady in Germany."

Ten Kids and Counting

My Uncle Russ lives with his girlfriend of over fifteen years, Michele. Together, they have ten dogs, each with different personalities of their own, and most of them were either abandoned, or shelter dogs. Eight of them don't like new people, or more specifically, me. Then there was their dog, Zeus, who thinks he's top dog, even though he's less than a year old, and clearly the runt of the lot. He acts tough when others are there, but is friendly with me one on one. And the tenth dog, is Benji. He is a smaller dog, with of all sorts of colors in his fur naturally. He's a blonde, white haired, grey and black dog. Benji is my favorite and I spent a lot of time playing with him. I wasn't a dog person until I met that one; he just brightens the world.

This trip was my introduction to Michele. Although my uncle and I are close, she and I had never actually met in person. We had spoken briefly on the phone when I would call for him as a child. She welcomed me into her home with open arms, demanded to fix the air conditioning in my car, and pay for it out of her pocket. We took the car to a shop, run by a man who looked like he lived in the 1950's, and lied like OJ's lawyers about everything. He said he could fix it, and it'd be ready on Saturday. When we came back, however, he showed me and my uncle that the radiator was broken too, a rock or small bird had gone clear through that and the AC compressor. He asked if someone had been shooting at me! Tuesday was our new day to pick it up, and on Tuesday, something else had been wrong, he'd gotten the wrong part. It wasn't actually back on the road until the following Thursday.

During the time my car was out of commission, my uncle and I saw many movies that were out that summer. We went to the movies more times together than I had in a few years prior. It was a way for us to spend time together doing something we did a lot when I was a kid and he lived in Lynn, Massachusetts. They really spoiled me while I was there; the car was paid for, food was free, and they went out of their way to make me feel at home. During the time my car was in the shop, my uncle and I took a two day trip to see the Grand Canyon and the Four Corners, which I missed on my way down. Michele stayed behind for work and to watch after their dogs. On the trip, he opened my ears to the masterful work of Kevin Smith's podcasts. *Hollywood Babble-On* was the soundtrack to our drive up. With that backing our road trip through the land of cacti, we drove all day north to the Colorado border. After talking about our lives, my parents and sister, and my comedic side, we arrived at the park leading to the canyon.

The Grand Canyon really was breathtaking; formerly carrying the water of the Colorado River, the canyon is left to look like a glorified version of where they filmed Mufasa's death. It feels almost out of place, like if it wasn't a national attraction, I might have thought it was in another world. Sure I'd seen many canyons before, but this one is shockingly large, overwhelmingly so. That night we stayed in a motel near the canyon, in a tourist area, where everything was absurdly expensive. The

McDonald's dollar menu became the five dollar menu, and so on. The motel, although expensive, did have comfortable beds and we slept well. We could only get a smoking room, which almost made my uncle vomit. That morning we drove west to see the Four Corners, driving along the canyon for much of the ride.

On the opposite side of the spectrum, the Four Corners is to this country as "How I Met Your Mother's" finale is to modern television. It sucks. A meter maid takes money for parking, and once you park, you've pretty much seen it all. There are the corners, sure, and where they meet are in nice stone and you can get your photo taken in the center of them all. I'm not sure what we expected to be there, but a crowded desert wasn't it. There is nothing jaw dropping about the corners.

****

After more films, board games, and meals together, the calendar turned to the fourth of July. My uncle had to work the third shift that night, and I looked for fireworks nearby while talking to Tyler and Shane about meeting in San

Francisco the following Friday night. Their flights had been booked, and their bags were about to be packed. We talked until nightfall as I walked a couple blocks away to see a great fireworks show. Once they started going off, I ended the phone call and soon after met a lovely woman named Kirstie, who detests Kirstie Alley because people assume it was her namesake. We talked as best we could through the fireworks, and had a great time doing it. She learned all about my trip, and I learned all about her life at home and about her artwork; she did wonderful sketches. We hung out afterwards for a while, and eventually ended up dating for about a month after the trip. It didn't work out, but she remains one of my better friends to this day. She made that brief part of the trip a little less lonely; Kirstie was the first person my age I'd seen in months and that I could call a friend.

The next afternoon, my uncle had woken up around noon, after getting home around seven in the morning from work. When he woke up, we went back to the movies one last time before I had to leave.

Mom

My road trip ended not with a bang, not with a spark nor a fizzle, but with the celebration of Mom's life and a high-tail drive from Phoenix to Reading, Pennsylvania.

I missed the first call, which was from my father around three that afternoon. I was seeing the most recent Avengers film with my uncle and when it ended and I turned my phone back on, I'd received a voicemail. The message was vague and somber,

"Hey Max, it's your dad, give me a call as soon as you can. Talk to you soon."

Naturally, after getting back to the house, I went to my room and called him back right away, I was worried and confused. He did not beat around the bush at all,

"Hey Max, did you talk to Grandad?"

"No, why?"

"Oh, I thought he may have called you too. The house got a call from him; Mom (my great grandmother) just passed away. He called the house phone and Mom (my mother) answered. I guess she passed away in her sleep, much like her sister, went peacefully." Everyone who ever knew her called my great grandmother "Mom." From her actual children, to the neighboring kids, to friends, and anyone else between, she was Mom.

"When are the services?"

"I assumed you couldn't be there anyways."

"Of course I'll be there, I have to go."

"Well, we'll call you when we know more."

"How are you guys taking it?"

"Well Mom is startled and shocked; I was expecting it for a couple years, and Zoe is sleeping over a friend's house, so we're going to wait until tomorrow to tell her."

"I'm pretty shocked too, I didn't know why you called me, but this was one of the last things I could've thought of. But I'll drive or fly out or something. I'll be there."

"Well alright then, I'll call you when we know more."

"Thanks, I'll talk to you soon, bye."

"Bye."

Standing alone in this room that isn't mine, I feel compressed and lost. So, naturally, I left the room and told my uncle the news I had just been given; he told me how sorry he was and asked what I was going to do. I relayed that I would be there for the services.

"But right now, I need to clear my head and go for a walk," I said to my uncle.

"Are you okay?"

"Yeah, I just need to think."

I walked out of the house, into the Arizona heat; it was now around 6PM and the sun was beginning to set. I lit a cigarette and began my walk. Once I turned onto the busy road by his house, I was faced with the aftermath of a car accident. It was between two cars, no one was hurt, just a fender bender. Cops were there, people were angry, and I wanted nothing to do with that. I had much more on my mind and walked through a parking lot to get around them. After the parking lot, there was a bench, for people waiting for the public bus. I sat down, dragged my butt, and for the first time, I cried about Mom.

At first, it was a couple small loose tears. I wiped those off my face with my shirt, smiled at them a little. But before I knew it, I had become the sobbing person on a public bench that made people look the other way. It became a brief hysteria; I could not control myself, and was so sad but so happy that I'd gotten to see her, and that she lived to be 96 years old. I was happy that she died like her sister, who, in my opinion, had the single best death I have ever heard of. I imagine I'll be jealous in my final hours.

****

Aunt Orie, about six years ago, had plans with her great-granddaughter. This girl, now a young woman, has been explained over and over as Aunt Orie's favorite person in the world, in her whole life. Well, she woke up this morning, got up, and spent the whole day with her. Orie was happy with this child and loved her more than most things. It was a sunny mid-spring day, just ideal weather for Reading. After the girl went home, Orie decided to sit on her porch swing that faced the street. And as fate would have it, on that beautiful evening, Orie fell asleep on that swing, and simply, never woke up. I don't know about you, but that sounds pretty damn perfect to me. Anyway, Mom didn't pass on a swing, or outside even, but in a nursing home, but still in her sleep, which still sounds just alright.

****

On my two day drive back east, I spent a lot of time talking with Kirstie, who helped me a lot with the passing of my great grandmother. She comforted me, and I would later return the favor with her own grandmother's eventual end. I made two stops on the way back, the first was at a cheap motel in Oklahoma City. This city had prostitutes like Boston had Dunkin Donuts, they're on every street corner, but not like you might suspect. These people, usually women, were delightful to speak with. We talked about the weather, the motel I was staying in, and other small talk. They were good momentary company, though I never asked them for anything, and the ones I met knew I wouldn't. They just said,

"I'll keep talking about whatever, but if someone comes over, I gotta work!"

During my stay there, I called Tyler and Shane to explain what had happened, saying I wouldn't be meeting them out in San Francisco after all. I apologized about that, and they brushed it off, saying it couldn't be helped. I was needed elsewhere. They still flew out and both fell in love with that city.

My second stop was in Spring Hill back with Erin who kindly offered me a room for the night. Running low on money, I started to worry about going back home. I made a couple phone calls, and my former employers, Frank and Nick, hired me back while I was still in Tennessee. This favor is one I would not forget.

****

After driving from Phoenix to Reading, PA (outside Philly) in about two and a half days, something I recommend you never do, I found myself exhausted and running low on gas, but finally at my grandparents' house once again. I met my parents and sister there; this was the first time I'd seen them since I'd left.

Unfortunately, it was also just past 3 AM. My mother had been waiting up for me; she hugged me, and we walked up to the apartment. I said hello to my dad and sister, who'd woken up briefly when the door closed behind us, then fell asleep on a cot in the living room with my family.

Once seven o'clock arrived, we were all awake and getting ready for Mom's wake. We put on our suits and dresses, our shoes, and our belts, and after a pot of coffee, we drove to the funeral home. Mom would have said parlor, not home. My parents, sister, grandparents and I were some of the first arrivals. We began milling about and looking at all of the photos and decorations of Mom that someone had already put on display for the family and friends of the departed woman. My mother was excited that a photo she had taken, not 10 years earlier, had made it into the display; many of us reminisced about how her old house looked, and how much I look like my dad who looks like my grandfather and so on. The priest arrived; he was seemingly timeless. He looked to be 200 years old; he was a hunched man with two canes wrapped around his wrists, with more wrinkles than hours spent awake. It was later explained to me that this man was the current priest at Mom's old-folks home, which I supposed made sense that he would be here, for her eulogy. I mentioned that Mom was 96 when she passed; someone at this funeral had said to me that when this priest was introduced to her at the home, she told the family,

"Yeah, we just got this older guy to be the priest." My grandfather and his brothers, and really anyone who'd heard her say this, said the same thing, "How much older could he possibly be?!"

Mom, of course, had no clue how old she was, what year it was, or really any concept for anything time related during her final years. She wasn't wrong though, the priest was actually born roughly six months before her.

After just about everybody had arrived, the priest began making his rounds asking everyone if they would like to speak at the service. Randy, Mom's youngest child, who is just a few years older than my father, jumped at the idea of speaking. When I was asked, I was not only a bit surprised he really was asking everybody, but surprised he asked me, because although Mom and I were close for many years, her children and grandchildren would've been first picks, or so I'd thought. I suppose he was an equal-opportunist priest. I was also excited and prepared for this chance. It seems silly and a bit selfish, but although I'd spent months public speaking, few parts of my family had actually heard it. This was almost a shining moment, although at an unfortunate scene. Naturally, I said yes, I'd speak after Randy had finished. Randy and I spoke a lot about this, and realized we were going to be the only two to be speaking that morning.

Randy, I quickly learned, is a great speaker, except to a crowd. When speaking publicly, Randy gets nervous and afraid, which seems strange considering he can always start a conversation with anyone about anything. Even my sister, who was grossed out by the corpse, bored out of her mind, and only wanting sleep and to go home, found herself talking to Randy for a good chunk of time. As it turned out, I realized Randy got nervous when, just moments before he was scheduled to speak, he walked up to me and said,

"Naw, you just go; it's all yours today."

Panicked and not quite ready, I tried to edge him on; he still backed down. Then, I guess something just made sense to him. When the priest said,

"Alright, and the youngest son would like to make a speech,"

I expected Randy to say something along the lines of, "You know what, I think I'm going to pass on that today, sir. Have Max take a shot at it!"

Instead, Randy changed heart and spoke for us all. His speech was heartfelt and, sure, he stuttered and stopped due to nerves, but also because he was choking up about the loss of his mother. He talked about how much he loved her and her him, his childhood a bit, and about how much he was going to miss his mother. The phrase "she's in a better place" was tossed around quite a lot that day, from Randy and everyone else.

My speech went a lot like this.

"I just got back to Reading from a road trip that lasted three months. I was fortunate enough to see Mom twice during this time. The first day I saw her, my grandfather and I picked her up from the nursing home. We were told that she had packed her things again and told nurses that she was leaving, which was sad because she wasn't moving out, but truly believed it. We signed her out and drove to McDonald's, which had become her favorite place to go. In the car ride, she talked about gibberish we couldn't put together, and once in the restaurant, my grandfather went up to order milkshakes for us all. While sitting there with Mom, she leaned in and told me,

"You know him," pointing to my grandfather, "He's like a father to me. He used to take all sorts of care of me when I was a kid."

"Mom, no. That's Jack, your son. Remember?"

Never while he could hear, but then while ordering, and later while in the bathroom and outside the car, she would exclaim, at me,

"That's Jack! He's My Son!! That's my son!!"

It was somehow sad and heartwarming at the same time. While together in McDonald's she would tell us about some basement we had never heard of, and reminisce about the building behind us. Years ago, it was the Ludens candy factory that she had spent most of her life working in, never breaking the two-dollars per hour pay. She had no idea why she was so familiar with the structure. She kept insisting that I was my father, and after we dropped her back off at the home, she would surely have no idea what happened that day.

The following day, however, my grandmother's best friend, Marie, had a concert at her church. We decided to take Mom along to it; that day we were faced with an entirely different woman. My grandmother and I waited outside while my grandfather went in to get her.

Once outside, Mom looked at my grandmother and said,

"Diane! I haven't seen you in I don't know how long!" and then at me, "And you! Two days in a row! When was the last time that happened?!"

She thanked my grandfather, by name, for picking her up, and when we arrived at the church, she spotted Marie across the room. Although they hadn't spoken in many years, she asked if that was Marie, and then promptly hugged her. She sang along to all of the 30's and 40's songs that the group sang, and couldn't have been happier or more in her element. Afterwards, we went out for a late lunch at a diner. My grandparents had offered to pay and when asked what she wanted, Mom had trouble settling on anything. When we suggested chicken fingers, since she'd always liked those, she responded with,

"No! Oh, no. No way, can you believe they charge six dollars for that plate? I could never ask you to pay that much."

Although she knew what was going on that day, she didn't understand money. Further, she still insisted I was my father, but over all, she knew everything that was going on. After lunch we dropped her off at the home, and went to Marie's house to play cards. That was the last time I would see Mom alive.

So, I guess it isn't her warm heart, or her house on Linden street, or her almost dangerous kindness that I'll miss most, but more her way of being so painfully old fashioned. Whether it be that the chicken fingers were too expensive, or the way she always had a refrigerator stocked with Pepsi, not because she liked it, but so that the mail and trash men would never go too hot or thirsty, or in the way that during the only time I stayed with her without my parents, she yelled at me, because,

"Boys don't do laundry!" That side of Mom is what I'll miss the most. Not to say that everything that she was wasn't wonderful, but that stuff always made her unique in my life.

Thank you."

****

After my speech, the service soon came to a close. At that time, we all quickly realized that we didn't have enough pallbearers. It was agreed upon that her six grandchildren should carry Mom. My dad and aunt could do it, and so could Randy's children. But my cousin Johnny couldn't be there and Wendy was unable to lift more than a certain amount. I was asked if I would be a bearer and said yes, and when no one else could Randy also stood in. The idea of this seems morbid to me, but he didn't seem to mind. For the first time, maybe ever, the six of us were alone together in a room. We had a good time laughing about Mom and about life overall, but what made us smile the widest, was watching my grandfather behave. He loved my grandmother dearly, but he also loved to flirt with blondes. We watched him talking to a worker at the funeral home and at least three times, she went to go help people with Mom and he would jump in front of her to try keeping her attention. That made us all smile.

Following the hearse to the graveyard, we learned that Mom was to be buried in a plot that was currently across the way from an old car show. As she was receiving her last religious service, the music of the car show changed to a loud saxophone-driven strip club-scene music that surely is found in a Tarantino film. The music blared over the pastor, who noted that it was silly. My father and I couldn't stop laughing, and my mother kept kicking us. I suppose that we didn't feel badly about it because Mom would have thought the music was hilarious and laughed right there with us.

Mom taught all of us a lot about kindness, generosity, and well-being in the time we all got to spend with her. For those things and an infinite more, I say thank you, Mom.

Fare-thee-well

After the wake, I stayed with my grandparents for a couple days longer than my parents and sister. I didn't want to go back. That's why after leaving them, I prolonged it further, by staying for about a week again with Mike in Guilford. He and Joyce had since broken up due to her drug habits mostly, and he was interested in Catherine, from The Buttonwood Tree. I played his wingman during that stay, and we played more open mics than the first time. We also got high nearly every day, and I told him all about the road. It was a final hurrah for me before going home, going back to a day job, and ending my trip. Sadly, Catherine chose the other guy to Mike.

Once I did cross into Massachusetts for the first time in three months, I found myself, very appropriately, pulling into a gas station with a Dunkin Donuts in it, buying a coffee, and smoking an American Spirit outside, sighing, because I knew it was over for now. Smiling, too, because I knew I'd do it again. I then drove up to Lowell, through familiar streets for the first time in what felt like a lifetime, and snuck back into my radio station to surprise friends. They looked like they saw a ghost. They didn't know about Mom or anything else that'd happened. They just knew I should be in California, not there. We hugged, I crashed on their couch for a couple nights, and then did finally return to my parents' house.

Once home, it was nice to sleep in my bed, to eat home cooked foods again, and to be able to call Tyler, Shane, or Emily and see what they were up to. I was back in my comfort zone, which was something I had escaped far further than I knew. I was home.

Made in the USA
Middletown, DE
19 May 2017